Other titles in this series:
The World's Greatest Business Cartoons
The World's Greatest Cat Cartoons
The World's Greatest Computer Cartoons
The World's Greatest Dad Cartoons
The World's Greatest Do-it-Yourself Cartoons
The World's Greatest Golf Cartoons
The World's Greatest Middle Age Cartoons

Published simultaneously in 1994 by Exley Publications in Great Britain
and Exley Giftbooks in Ihc USA.

Selection © Exley Publications Ltd.
The copyright for each cartoon remains with the cartoonist.

ISBN 1-85015-506-2

Front cover illustration by Roland Fiddy.
Designed by Pinpoint Design.
Edited by Mark Bryant.
Printed and bound by Grafo, S.A., Bilbao, Spain.

Exley Publications Ltd, 16 Chalk Hill, Watford, Herts WD1 4BN, UK.
Exley Giftbooks, 232 Madison Avenue, Suite 1206, NY 10016, USA.

THANK YOU

We would like to thank all the cartoonists who submitted entries for *The World's Greatest KEEP-FIT CARTOONS*.
They came in from many parts of the world – including Israel, Romania, Spain, Mexico and New Zealand.

Special thanks go to the cartoonists whose work appears in the final book. They include Les Barton pages 7,
18, 25, 34, 53; Eli Bauer page 67; Stan Eales pages 20, 65; Stidley Easel pages 13, 35, 39, 57, 78; Roland
Fiddy cover, title page and page 50; Grizelda Grizlingham page 21; Harca page 61; Michael Heath page 14;
Martin Honeysett pages 44, 72 ; Tony Husband pages 4, 8, 15, 24, 30, 33, 38, 42, 47, 55, 60, 68, 70, 73,
75, 76, 79; Mik Jago pages 12, 27, 45; Larry pages 9, 26, 43, 48, 63; Peter Maddocks pages 31, 49, 56;
David Myers pages 41, 58; Sergio Navarro page 51; David Pye pages 5, 10, 22, 28, 37, 46, 54, 71, 74, 77;
Constantin Pavel pages 16 & 17; Viv Quillin 59, 69; Bryan Reading 23, 40; Colin Whittock pages 6, 11, 19,
29, 32, 36, 52, 62, 64, 66.

Every effort has been made to trace the copyright holders of cartoons in this book. However, any error will
gladly be corrected by the publisher for future printings.

THE WORLD'S GREATEST

KEEP-FIT

CARTOONS

EDITED BY
Mark Bryant

 EXLEY
NEW YORK · WATFORD, UK

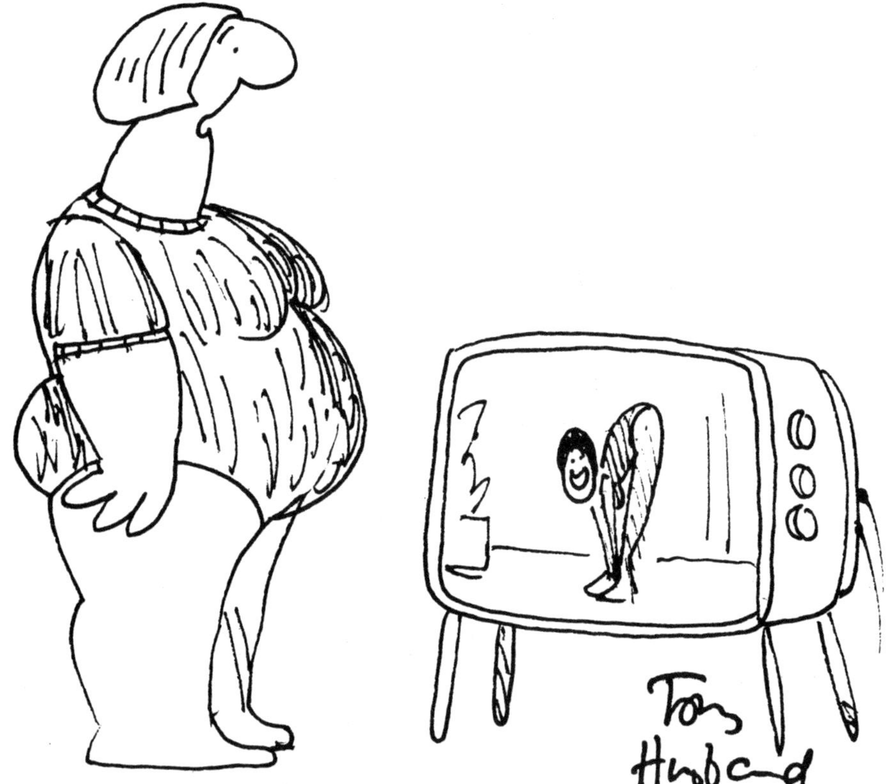
Tom Husband

"Touch my toes? What toes?"

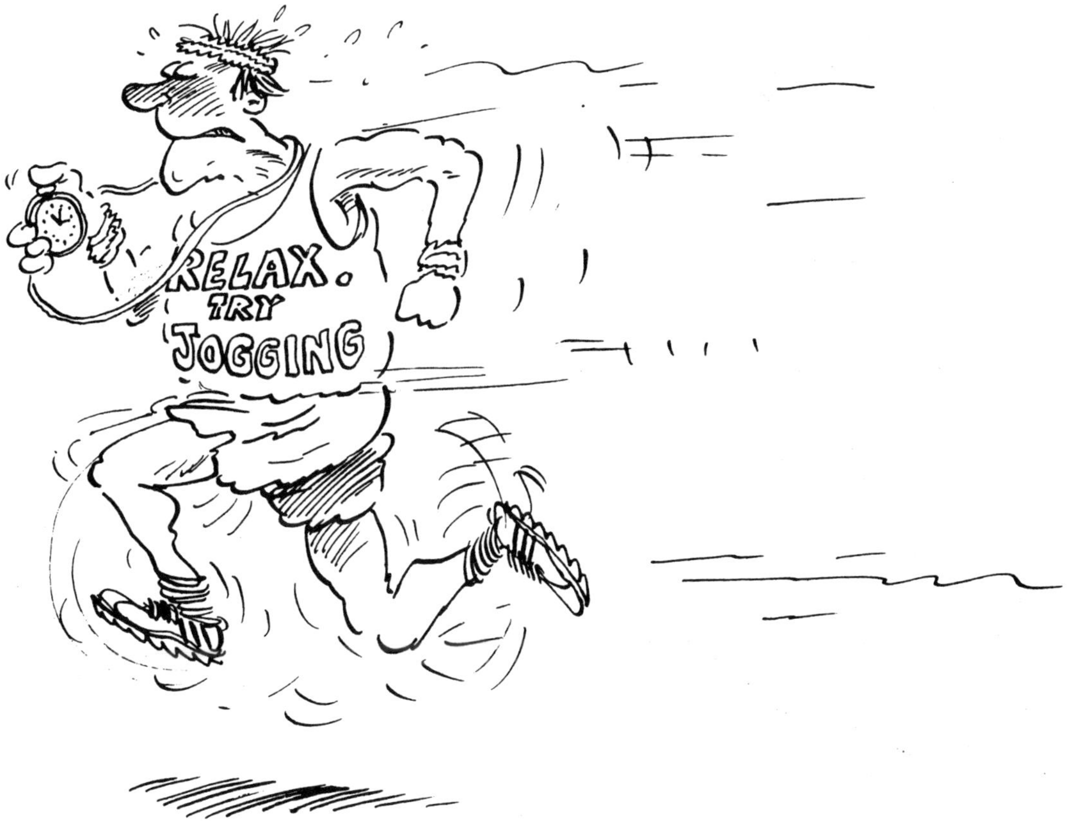
RELAX.
TRY
JOGGING

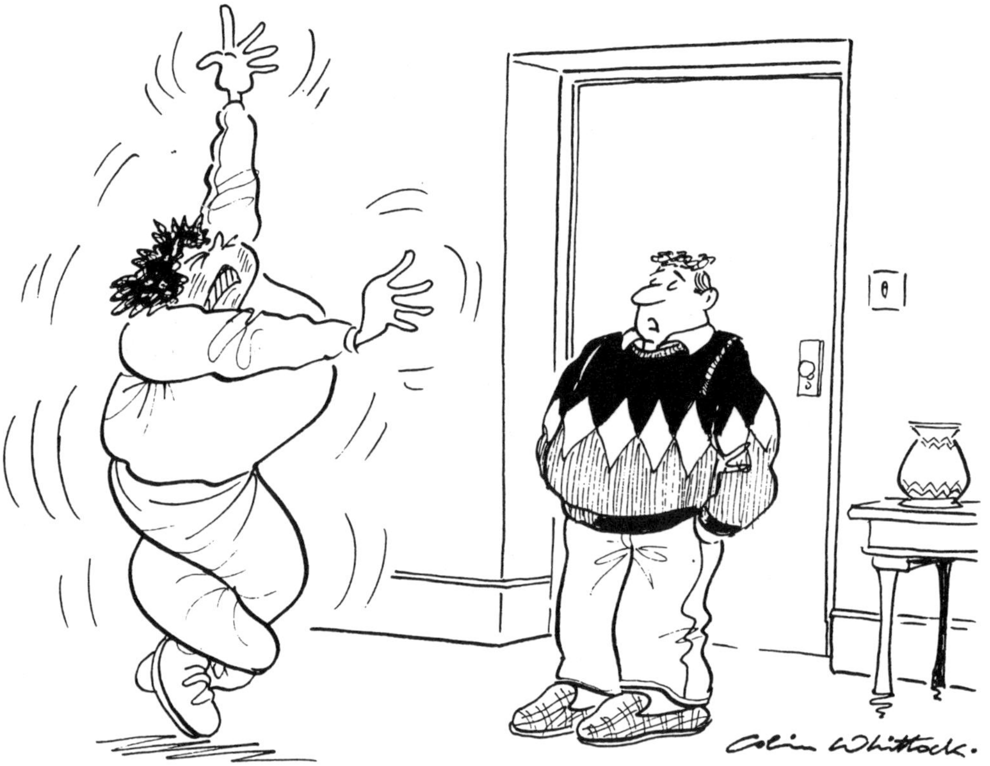
Colin Whittock.

"Some things just don't mix, Sharon, and you and aerobics . . ."

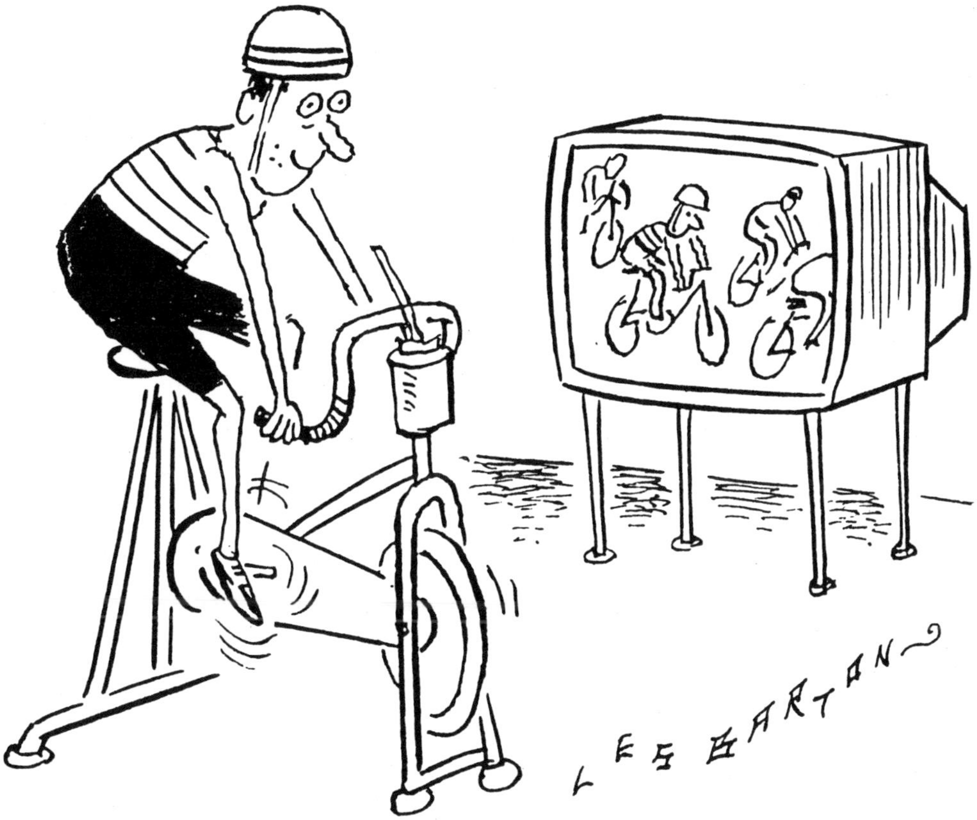
LES BARTON

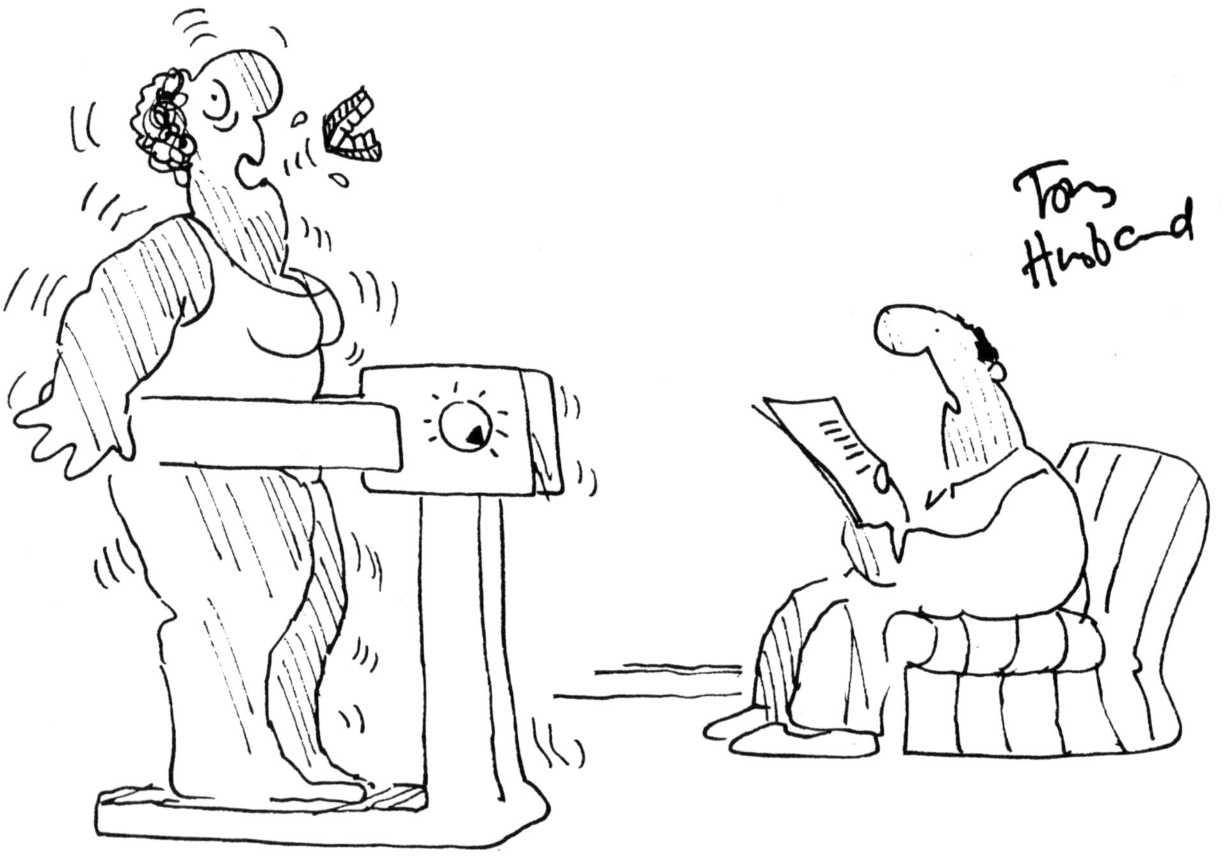
Tony Husband

"Is it on too high, honey?"

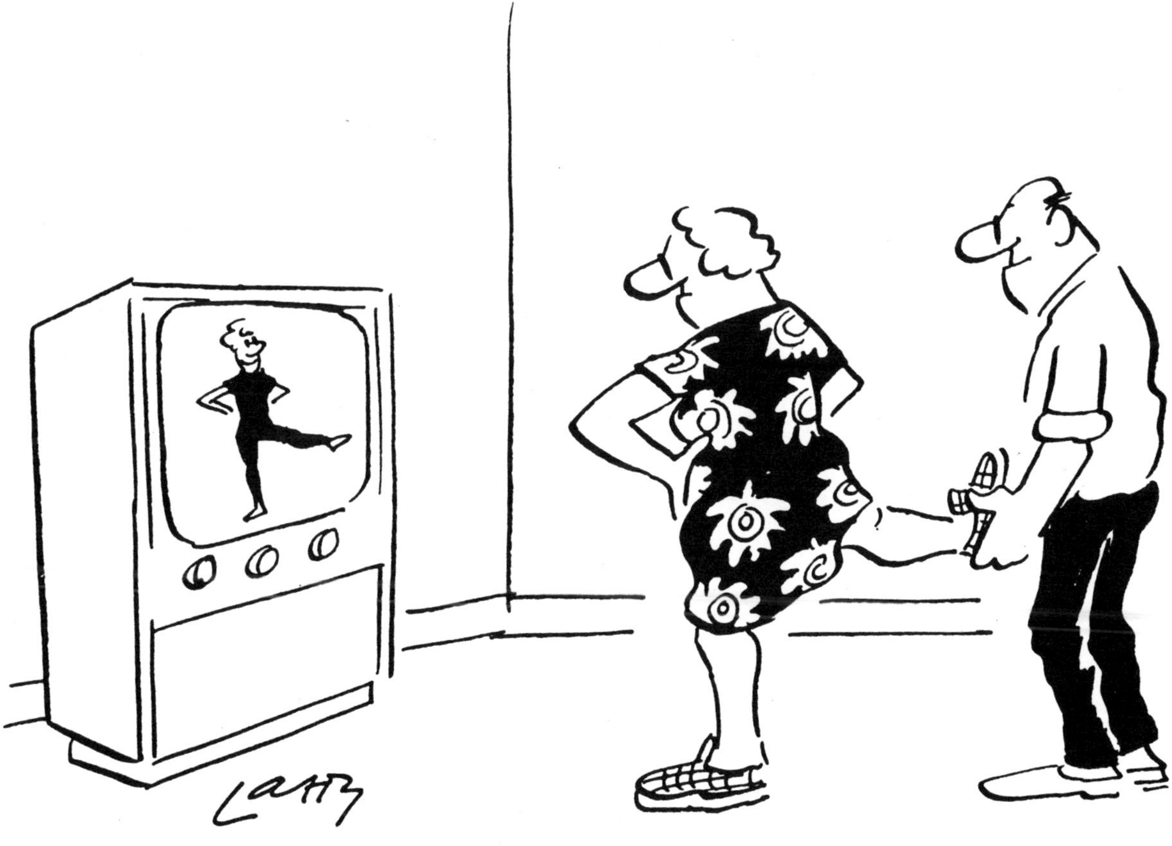
Larry

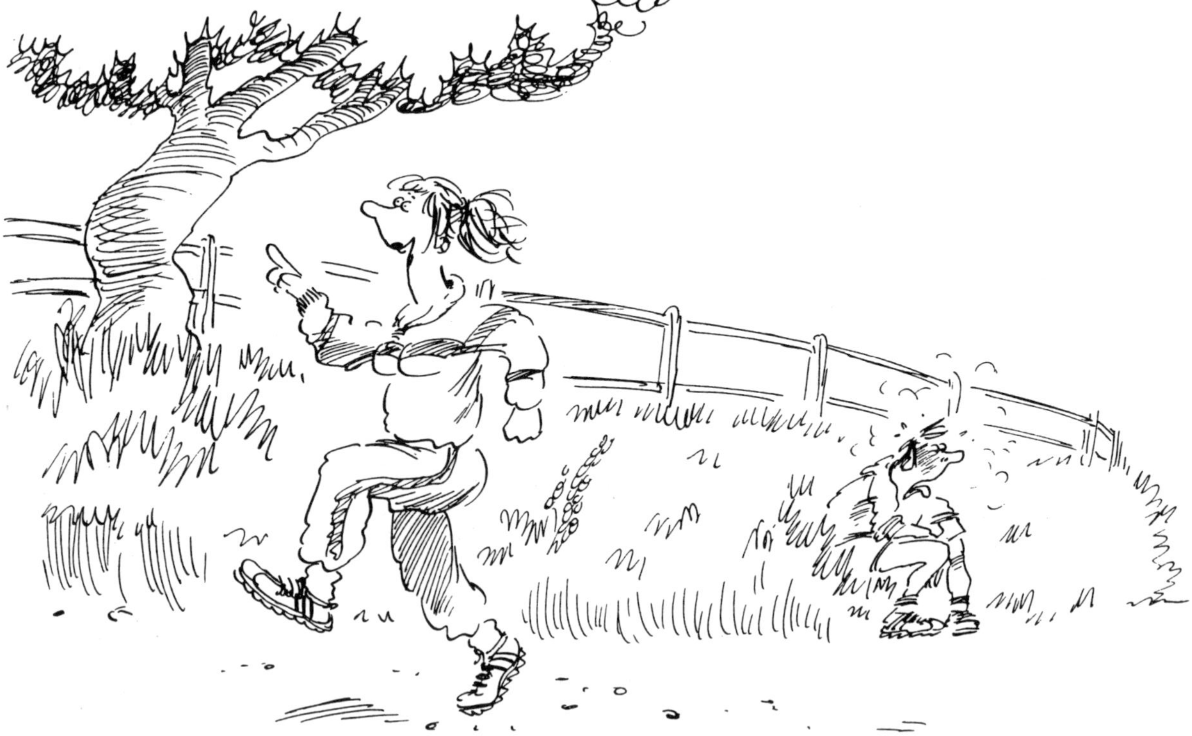

"Knees up, Sweetie! Only another five miles!"

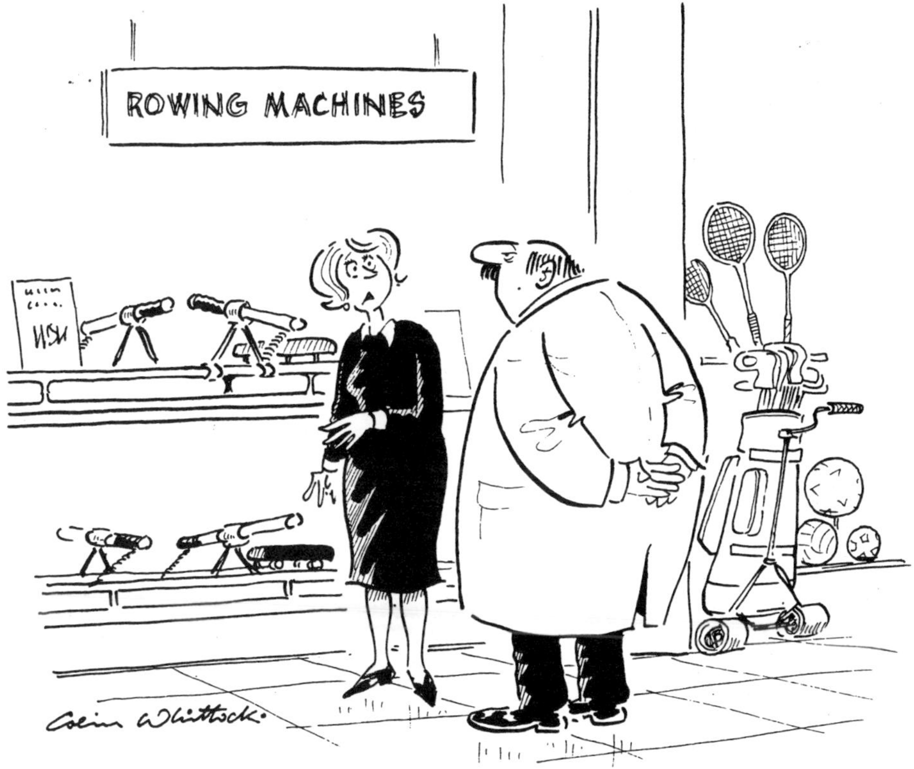
ROWING MACHINES

"I'm sorry, sir, we don't do one fitted with an outboard motor . . ."

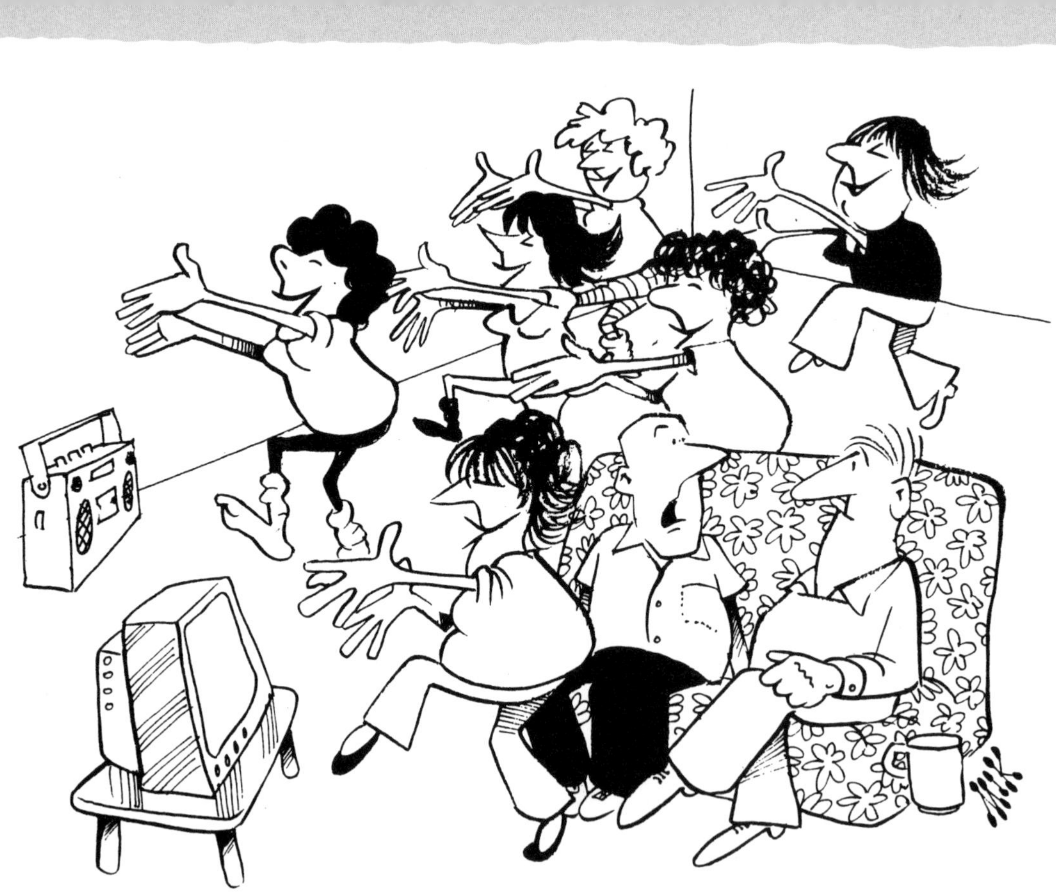

"I preferred her bridge evenings."

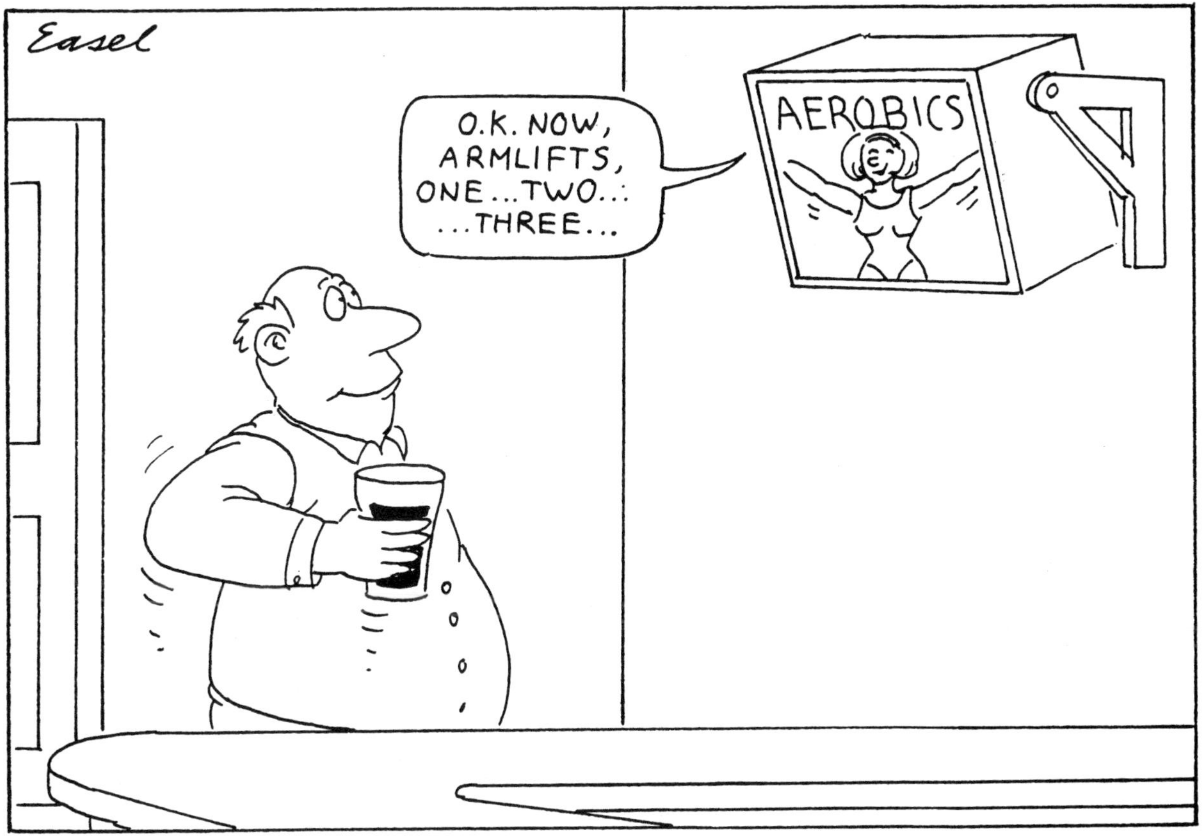
Easel
O.K. NOW, ARMLIFTS, ONE...TWO... ...THREE...
AEROBICS

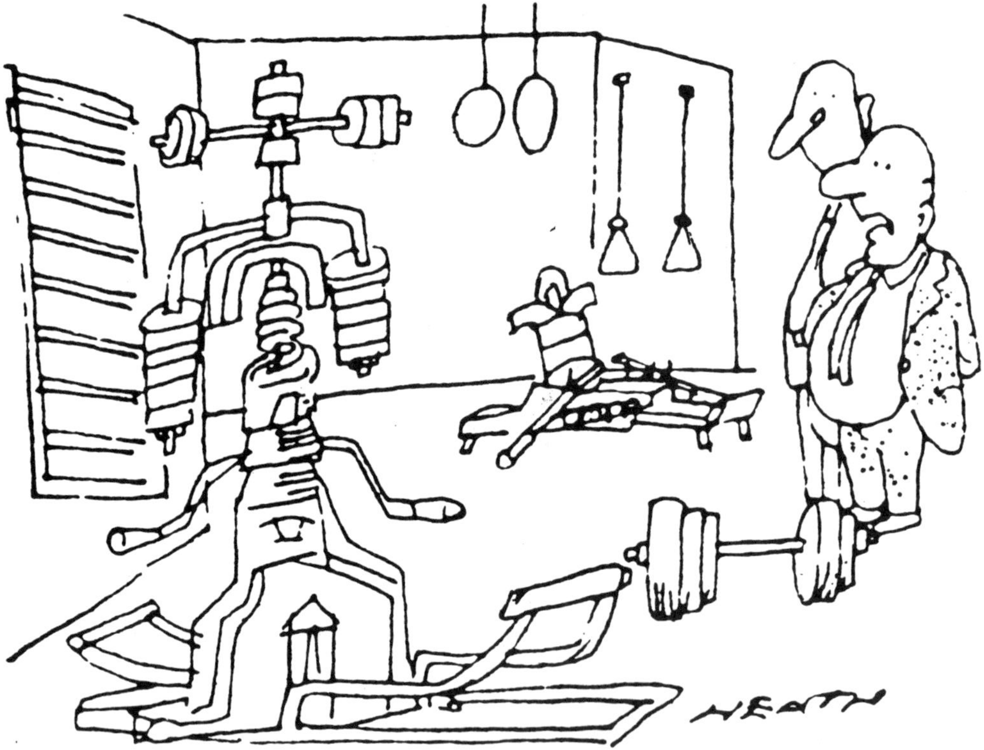
HEATH

"The trouble is, I can never get fit enough to use the equipment."

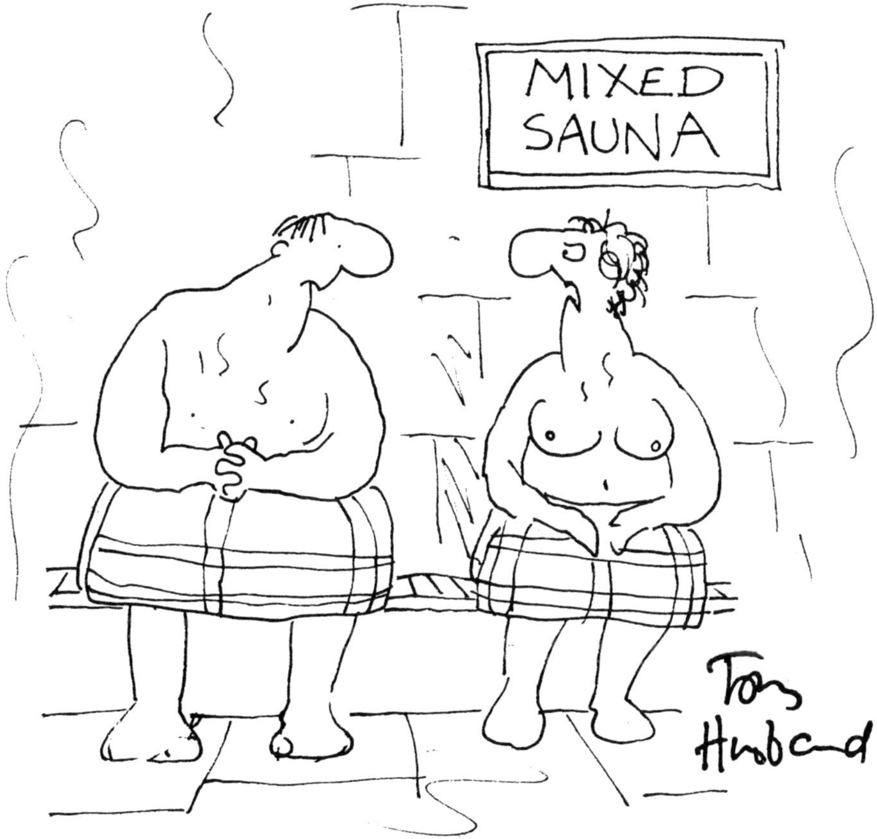
MIXED
SAUNA
Tony
Husband

"Oi! Contemplate your own navel!"

1.

2.

3.

C. PAVEL

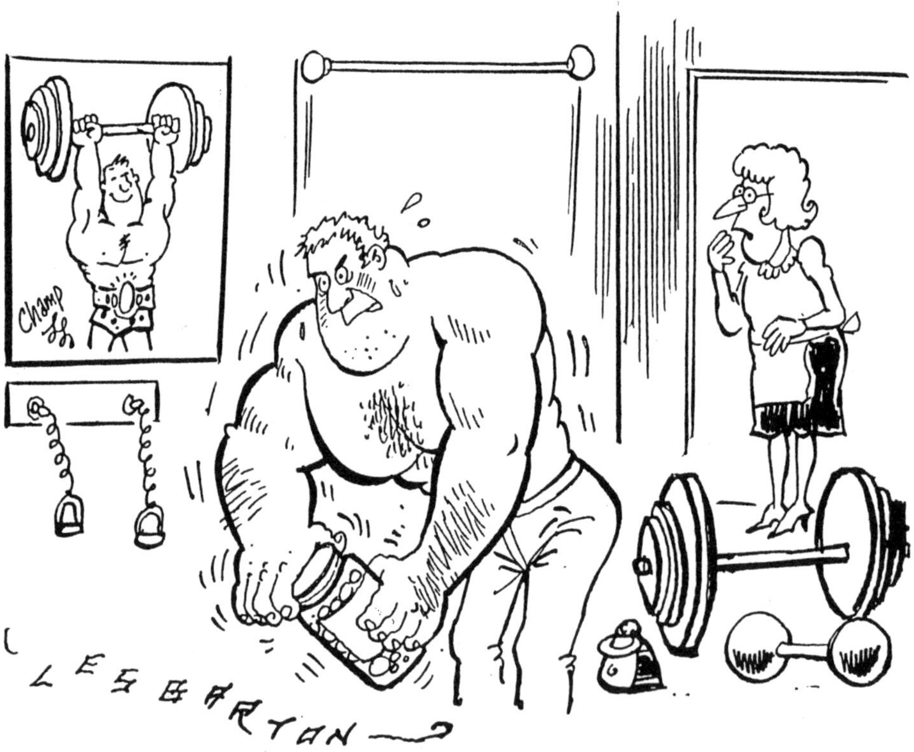
Champ
LESBARTON

"Shall I do it?"

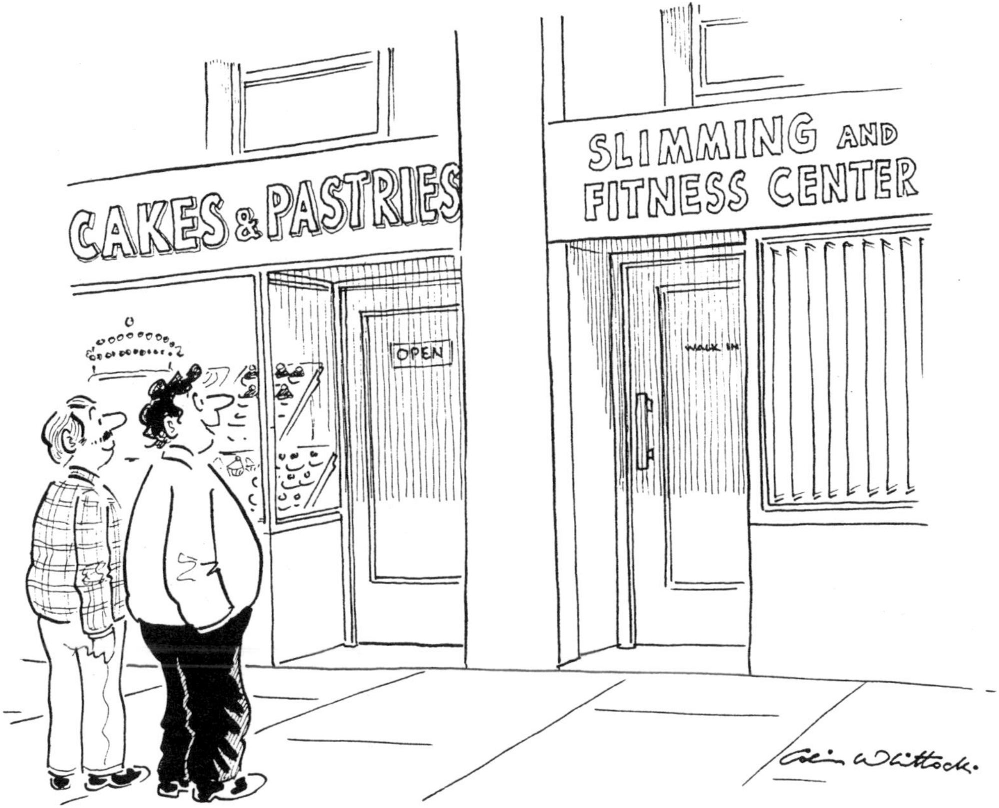
CAKES & PASTRIES
OPEN
SLIMMING AND
FITNESS CENTER
Colin Whittock.

"Business has been great since I bought both shops."

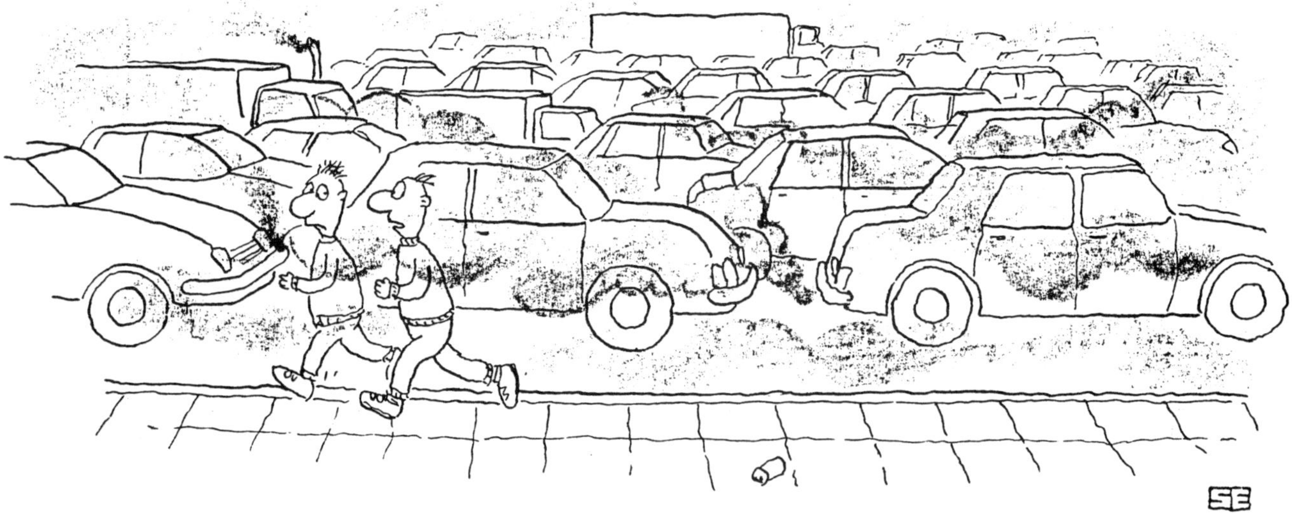
SE

"I'm going back to being a slob, Roger. It's more healthy."

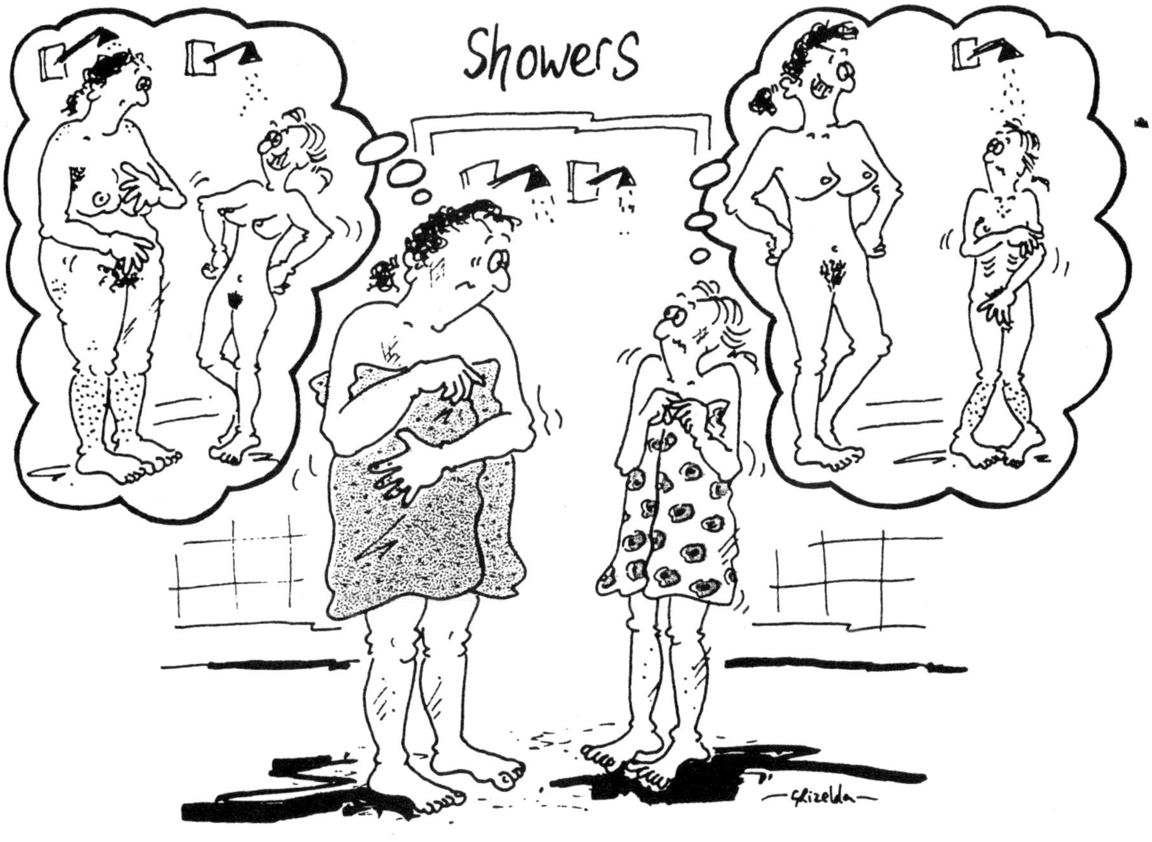
Showers
Grizelda

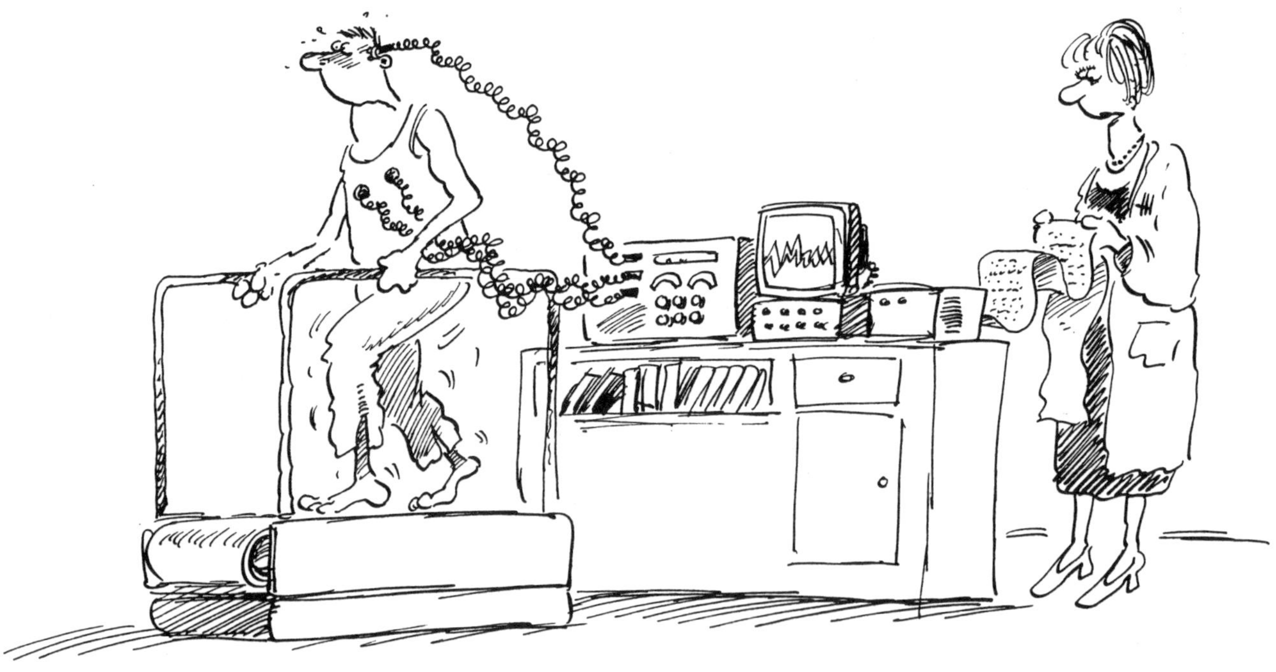

"I'm not saying you're out of condition, but the machine appears to be laughing!"

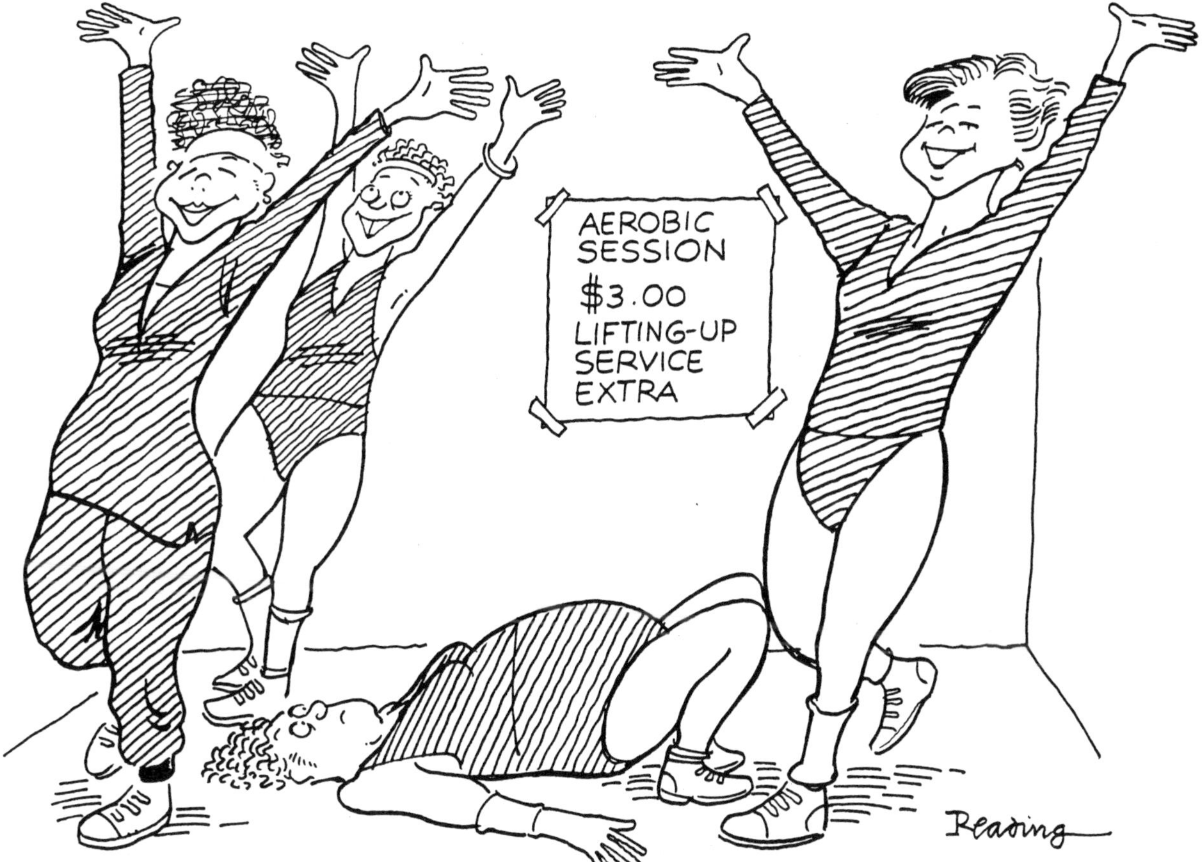
AEROBIC
SESSION
$3.00
LIFTING-UP
SERVICE
EXTRA
Reading

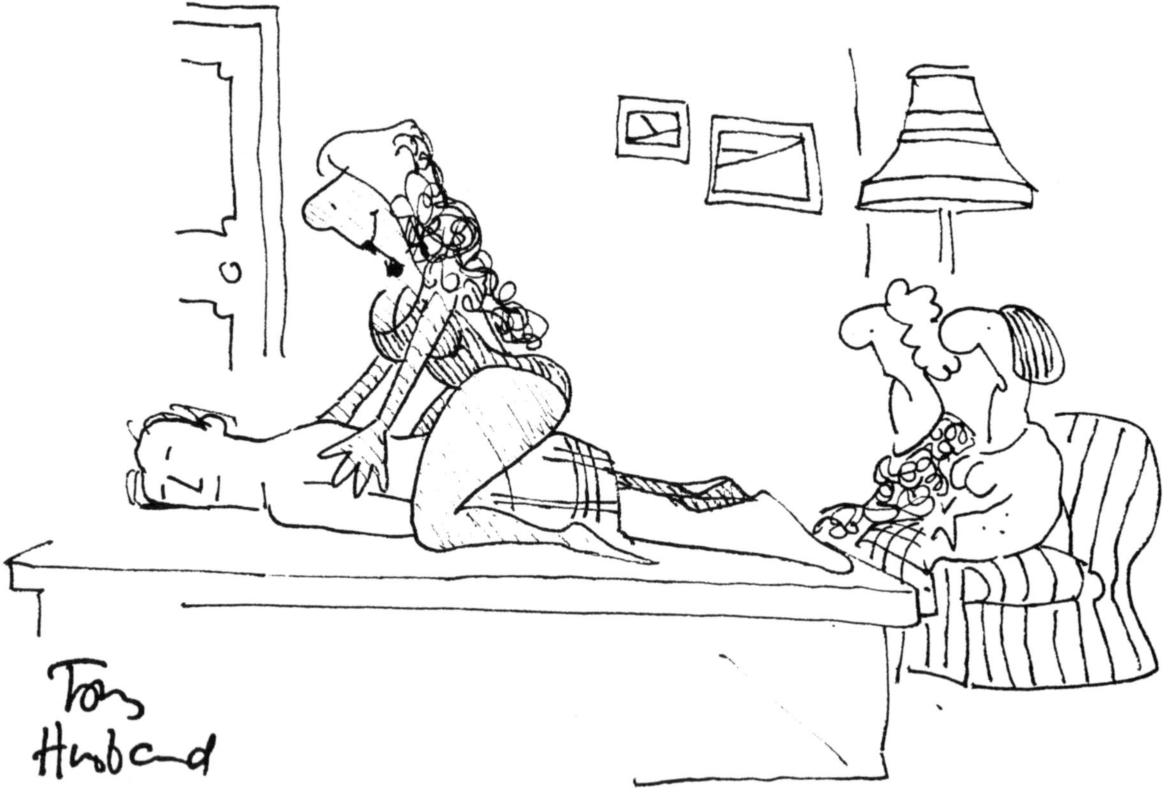
Tony Husband

"She comes once a week. He says she does wonders for his back."

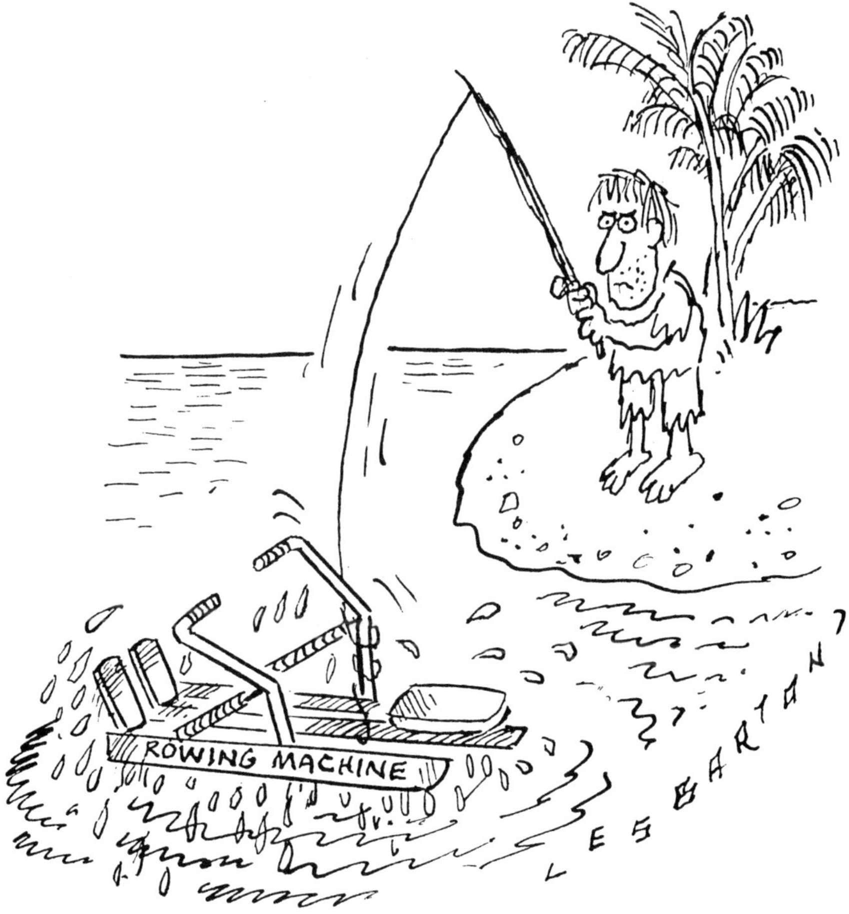
ROWING MACHINE
LES BARTON

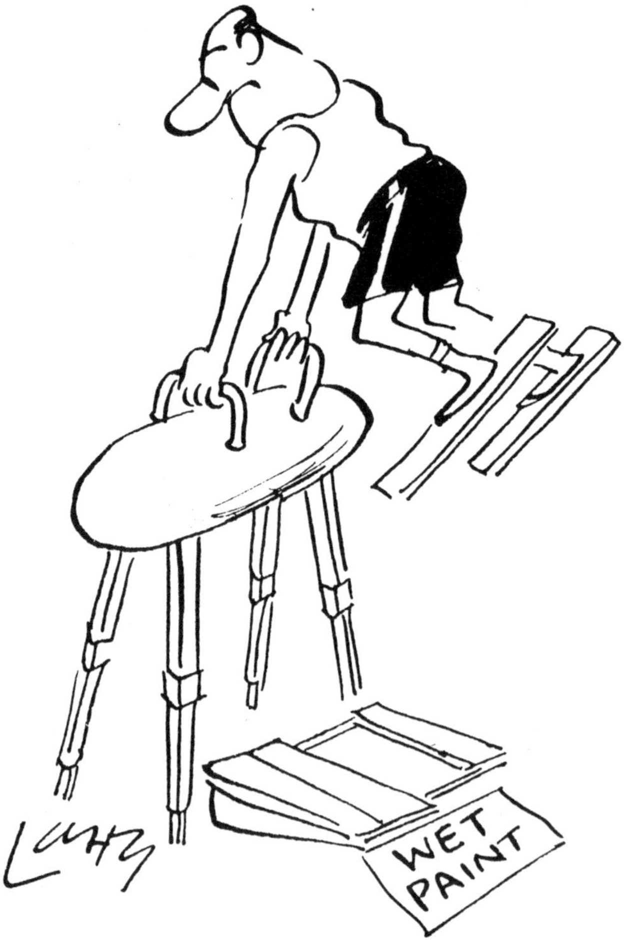
WET PAINT

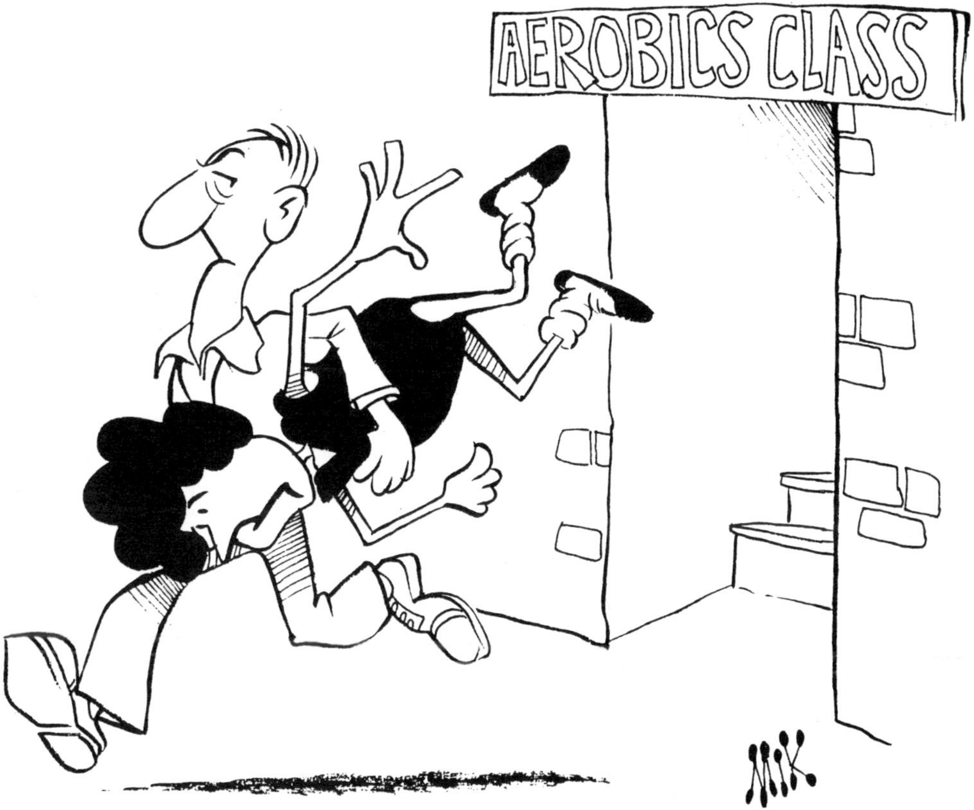
AEROBICS CLASS
MIK

"They told me that the second lesson is much easier."

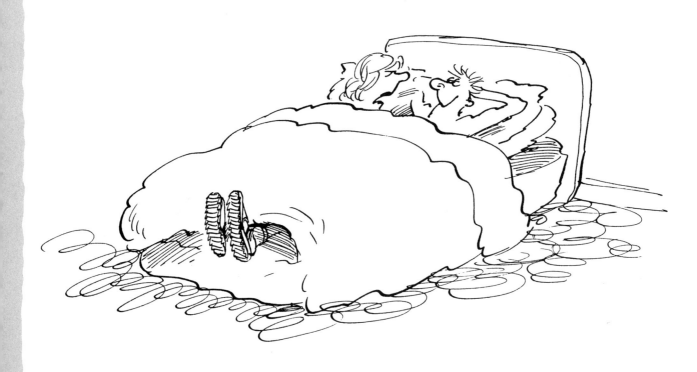

*"I know it's supposed to be the equivalent of a two-mile run,
but there's no need to dress for the part!"*

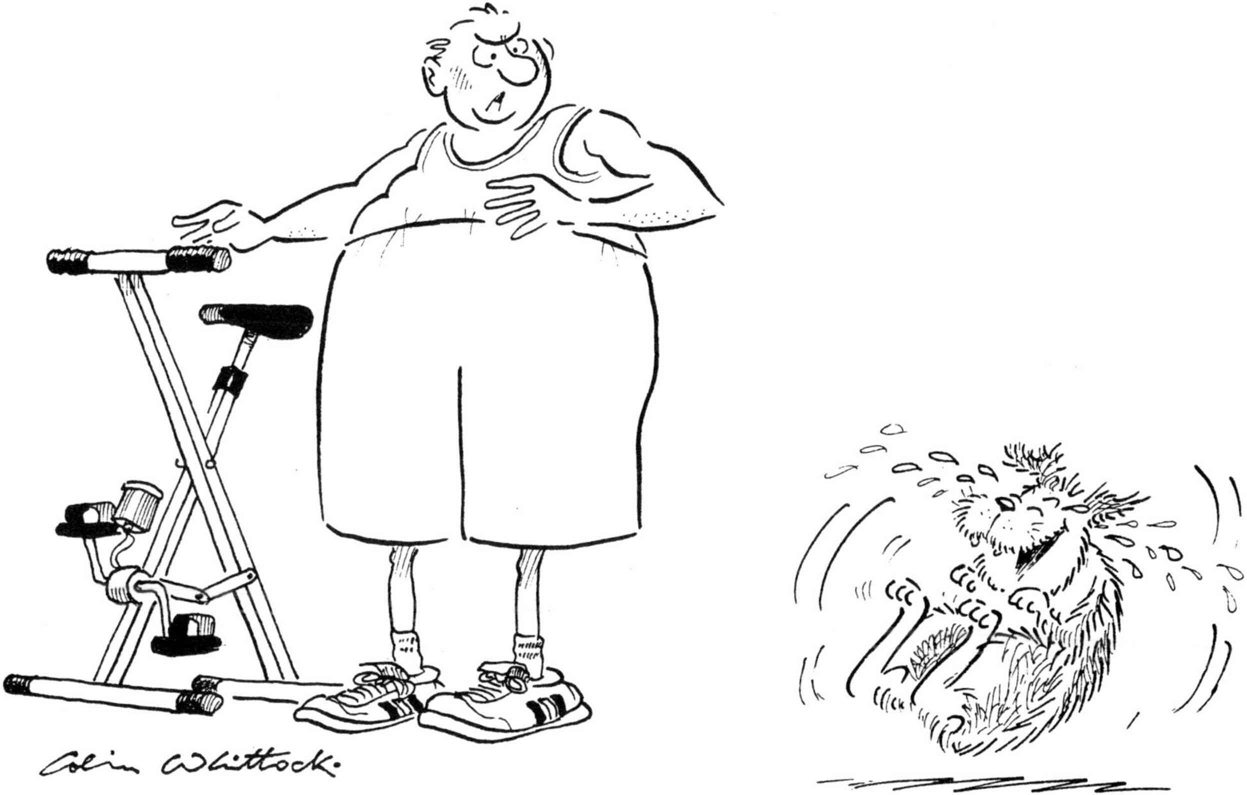
Colin Whittock

"Do you mind . . . !"

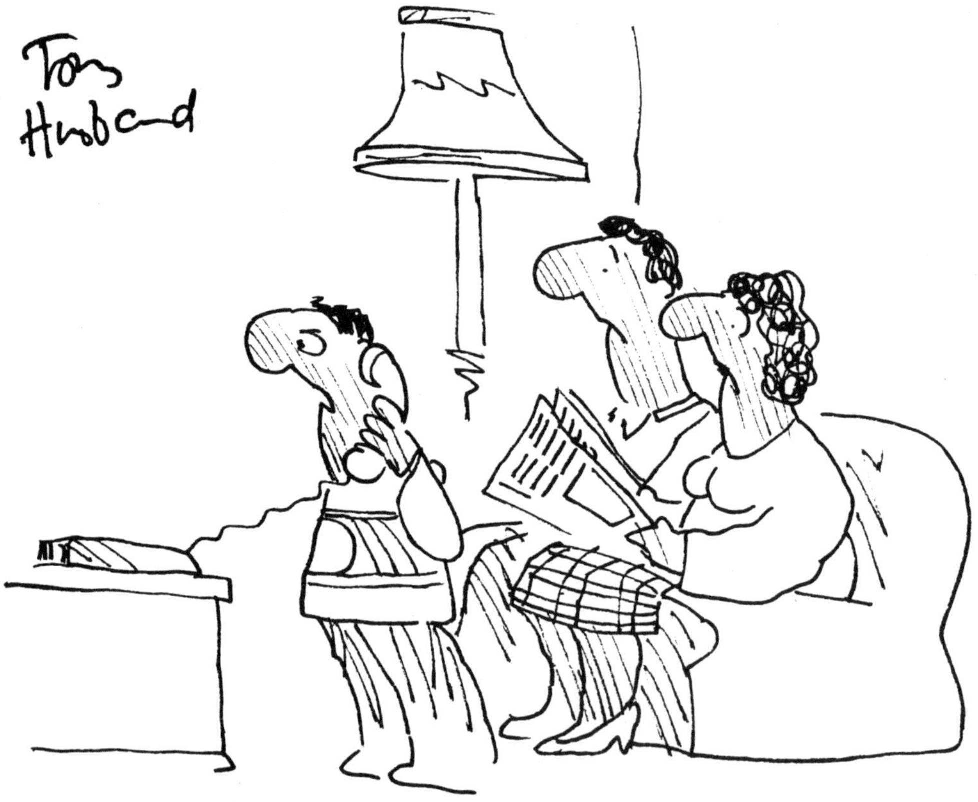

"No way! My mother's a bigger tub of lard than your mother!"

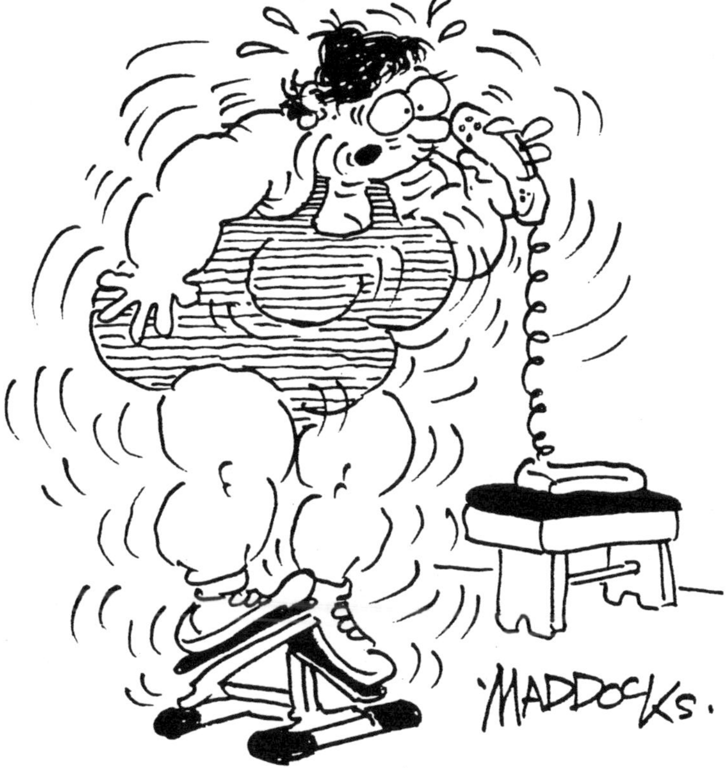
MADDOCKS.

"I can stop the machine, but I can't stop the wobble!"

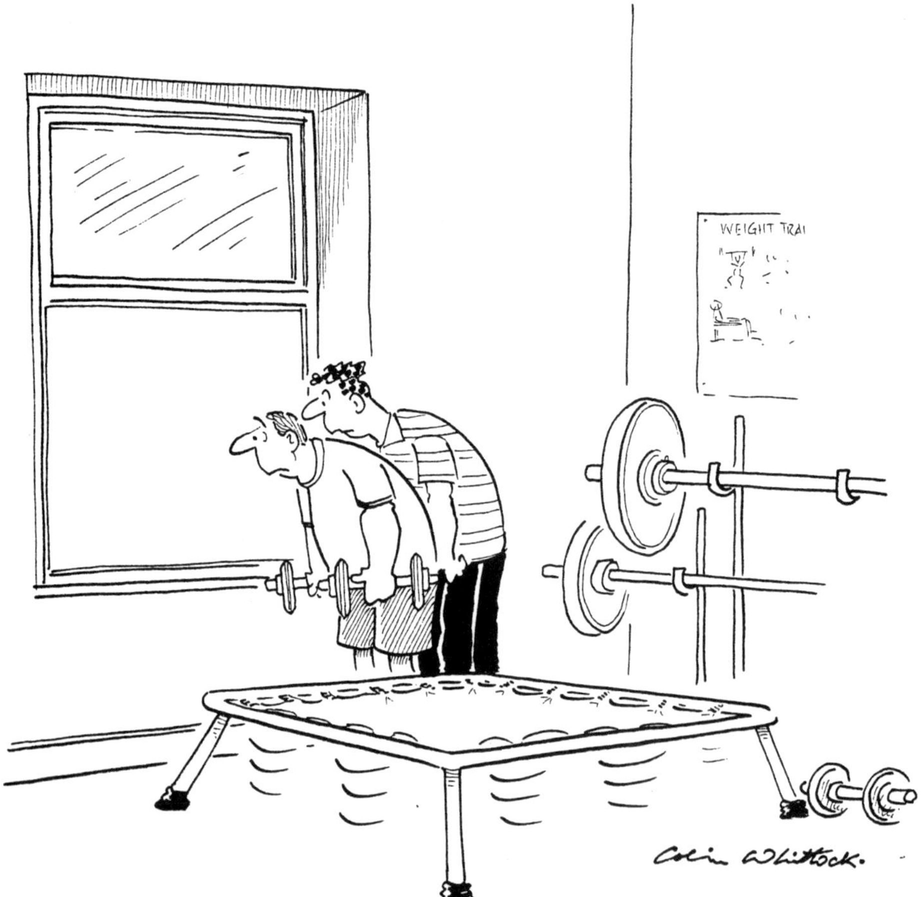
WEIGHT TRAI
Colin Whittock.

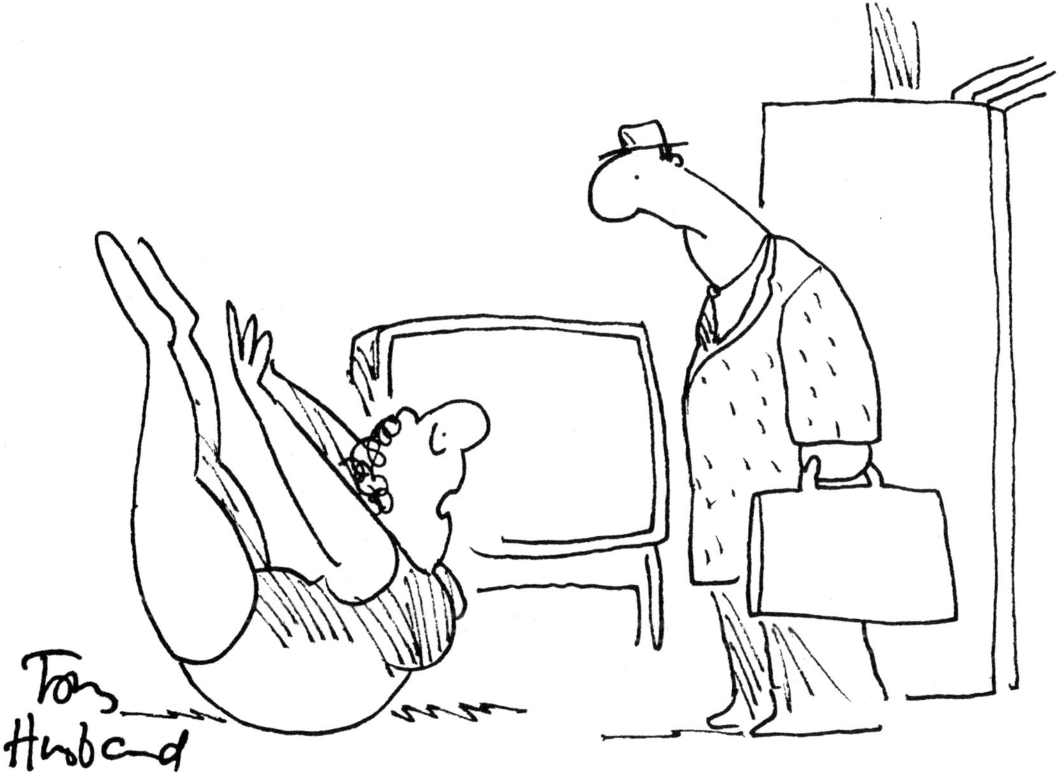
Tony Husband

"I was watching a Jane Fonda workout video this morning and got stuck."

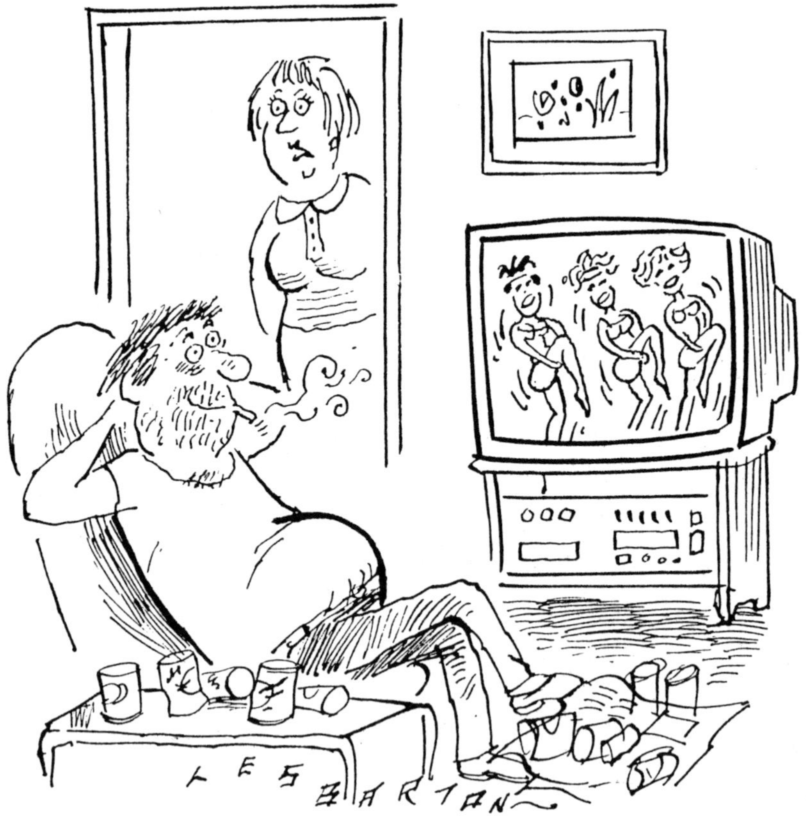
LES BARTON

"You're getting to be a proper health crank!"

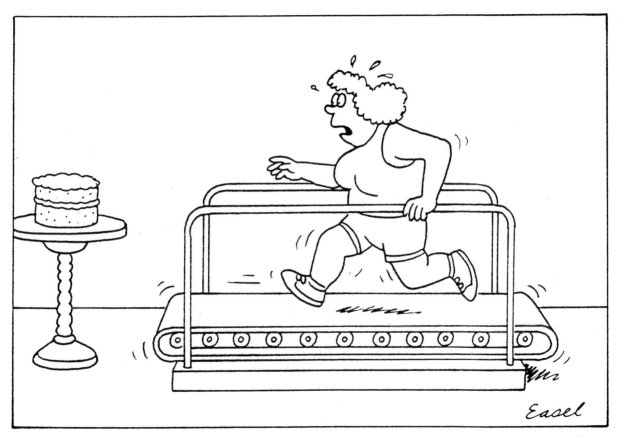

Easel

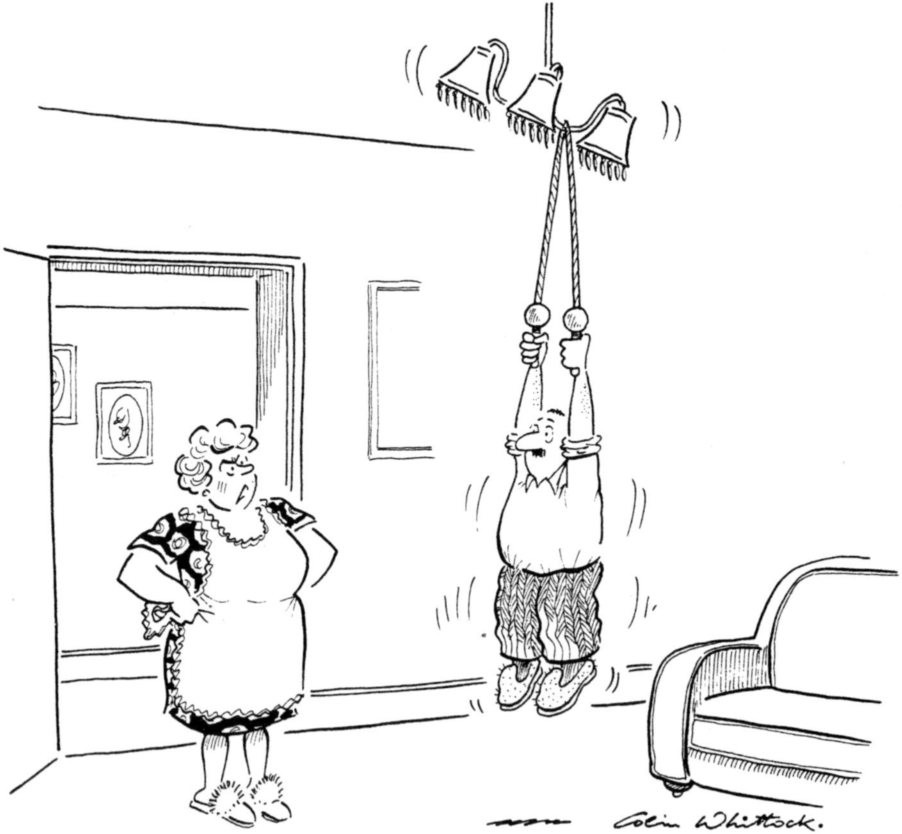
Colin Whittock.

"Not again . . . ?"

"I can't stand show-offs. I'd sock him one if I could only catch him!"

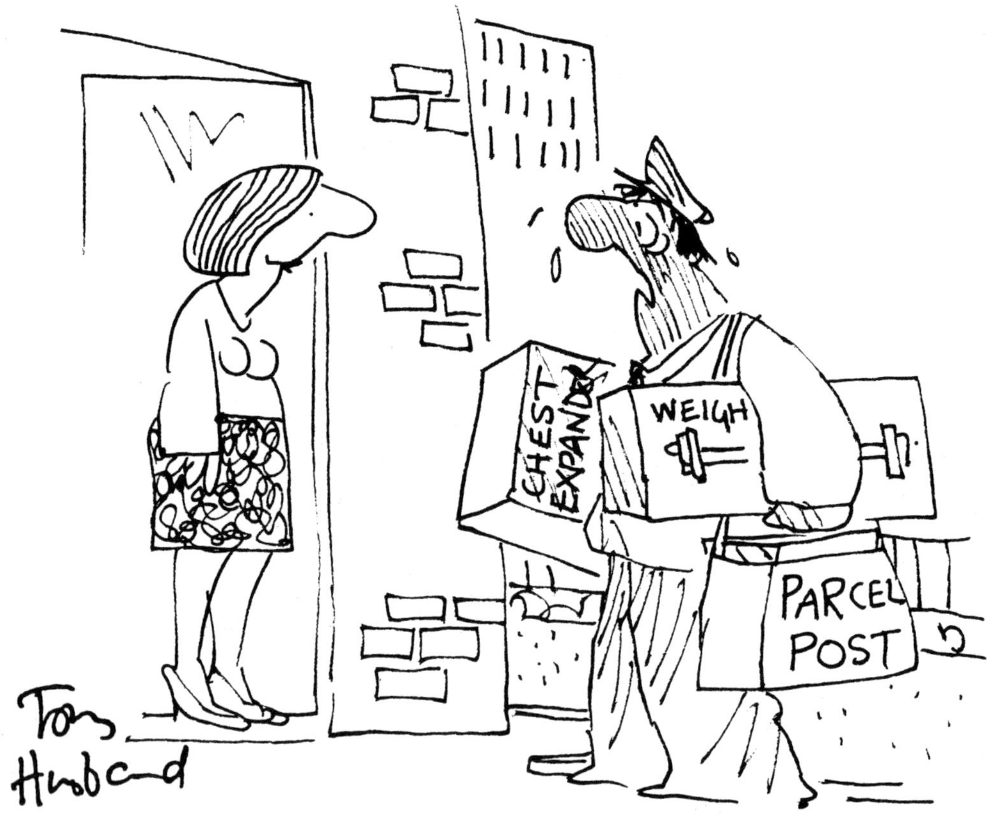
CHEST EXPANDER
WEIGH
PARCEL POST
Tom Hubbard

"Gasp – I'll be glad when you've got the full gym!"

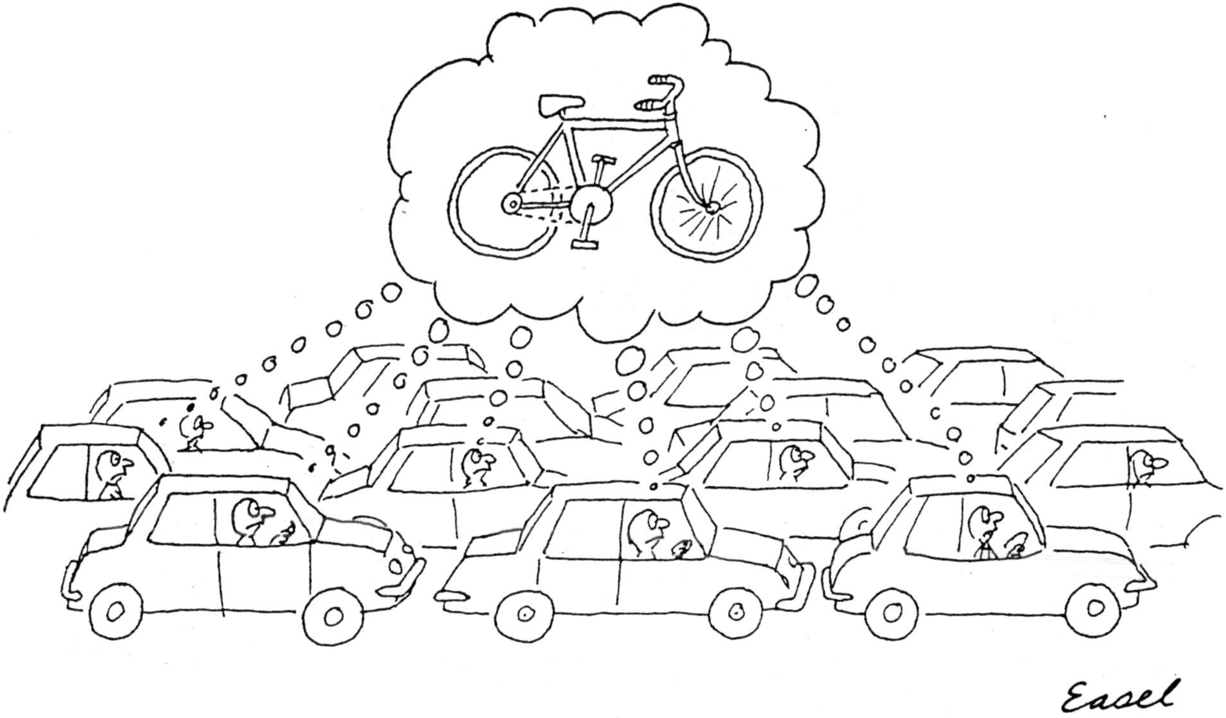
Easel

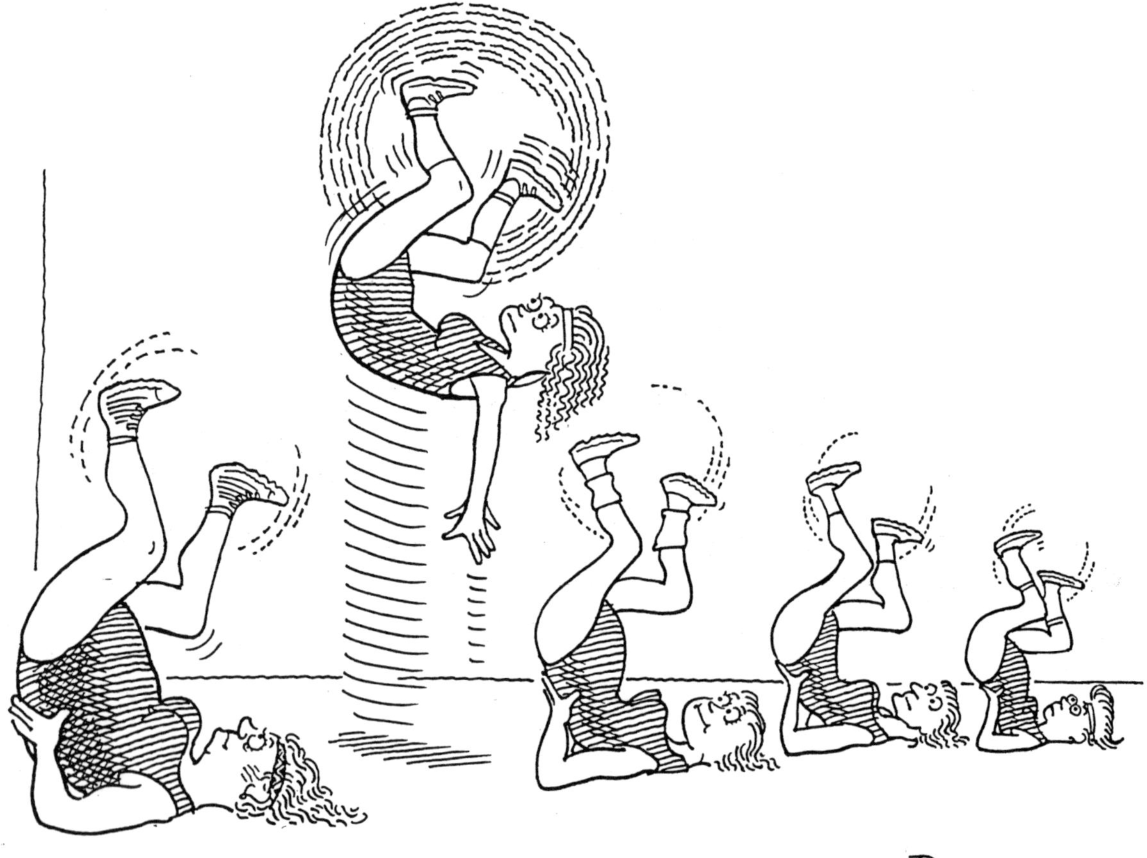
Reading

"George watches his weight very carefully."

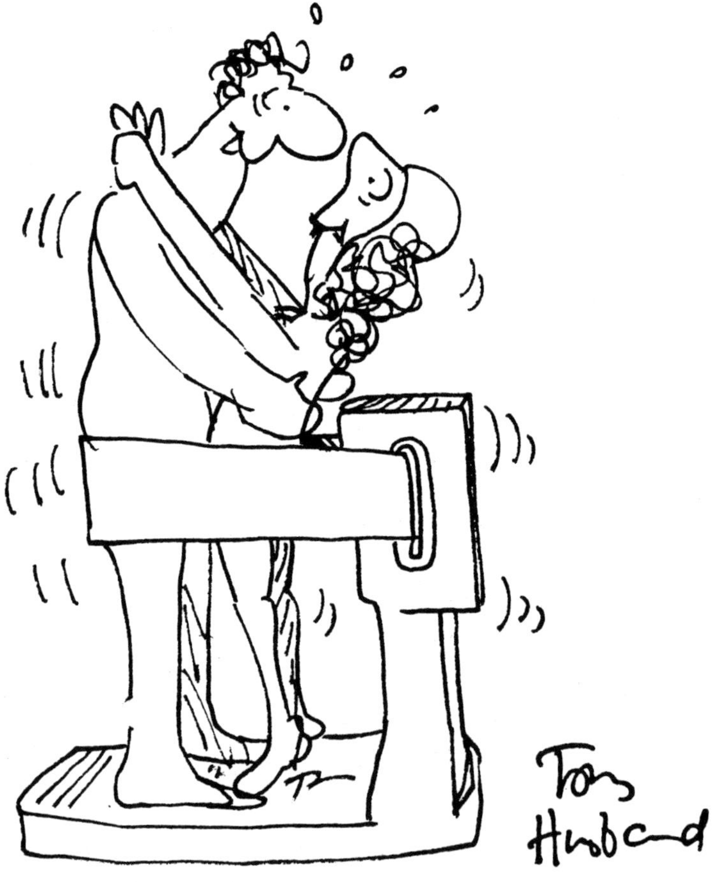
Tom
Hubbard

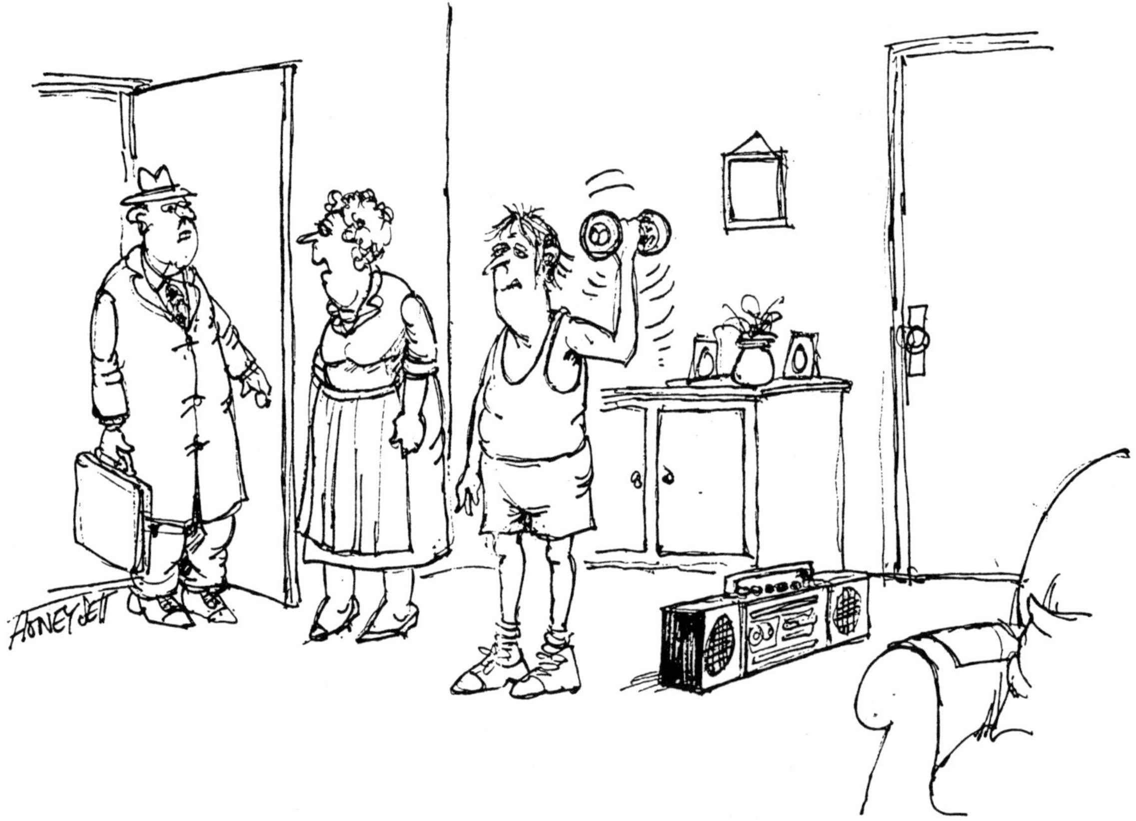
HONEYSETT

"He's in training to carry his radio."

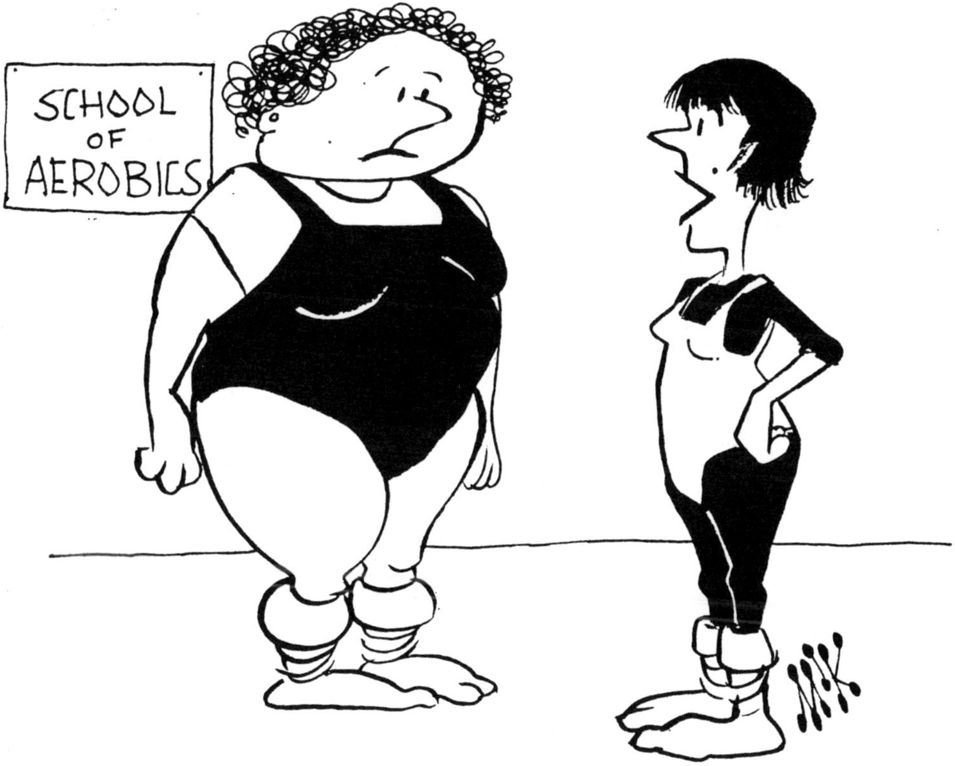
SCHOOL
OF
AEROBICS

"Well, there's nothing I like more than a challenge, Mrs Forbes."

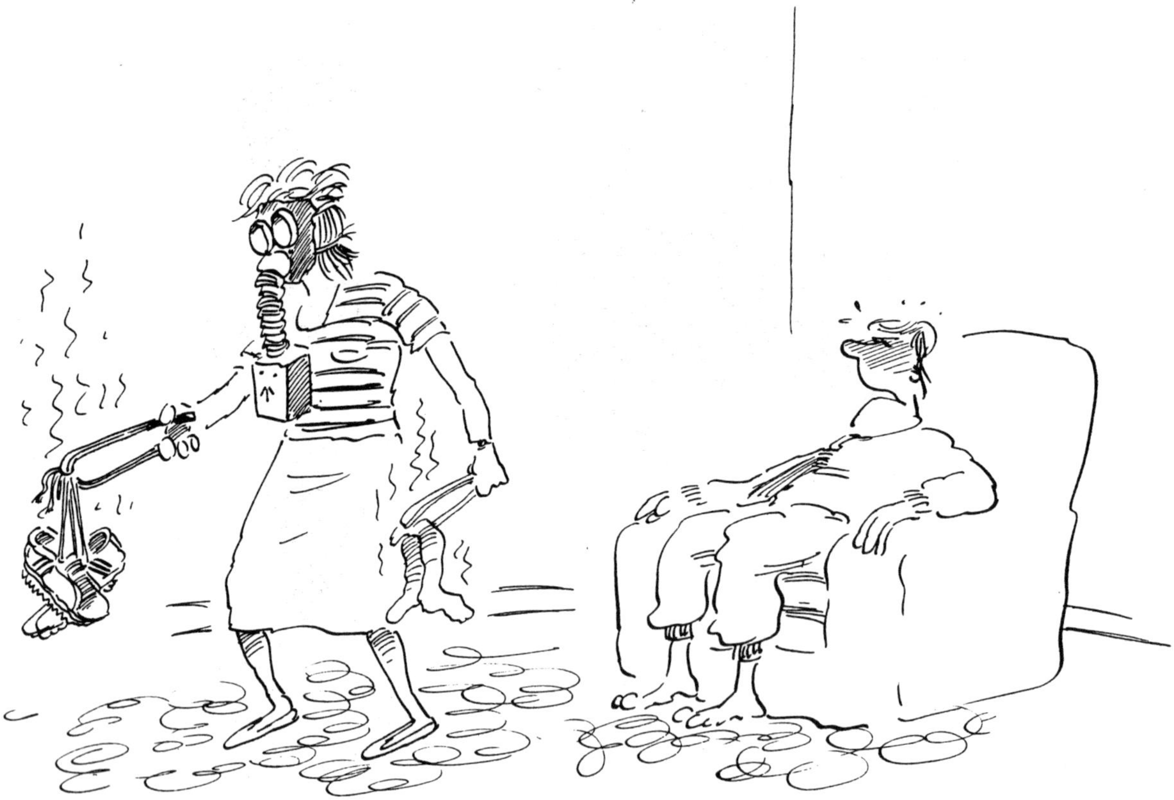

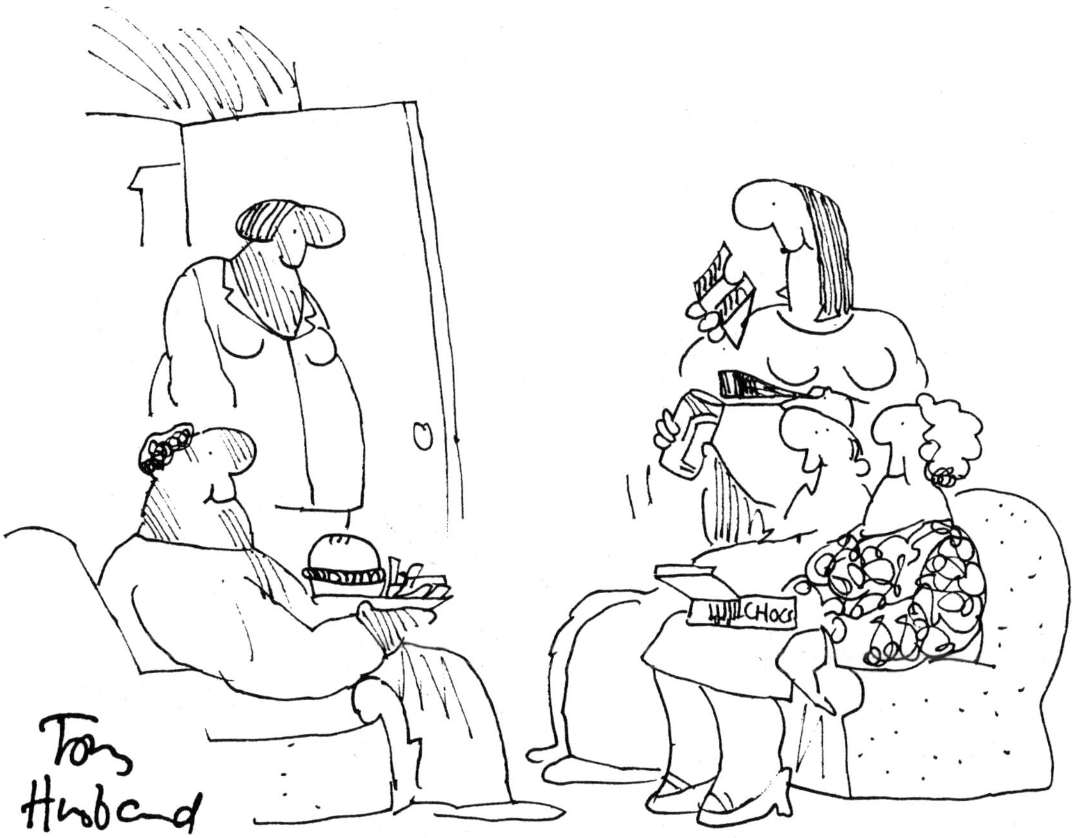
CHOCS

"Welcome to the Keep Fat Club!"

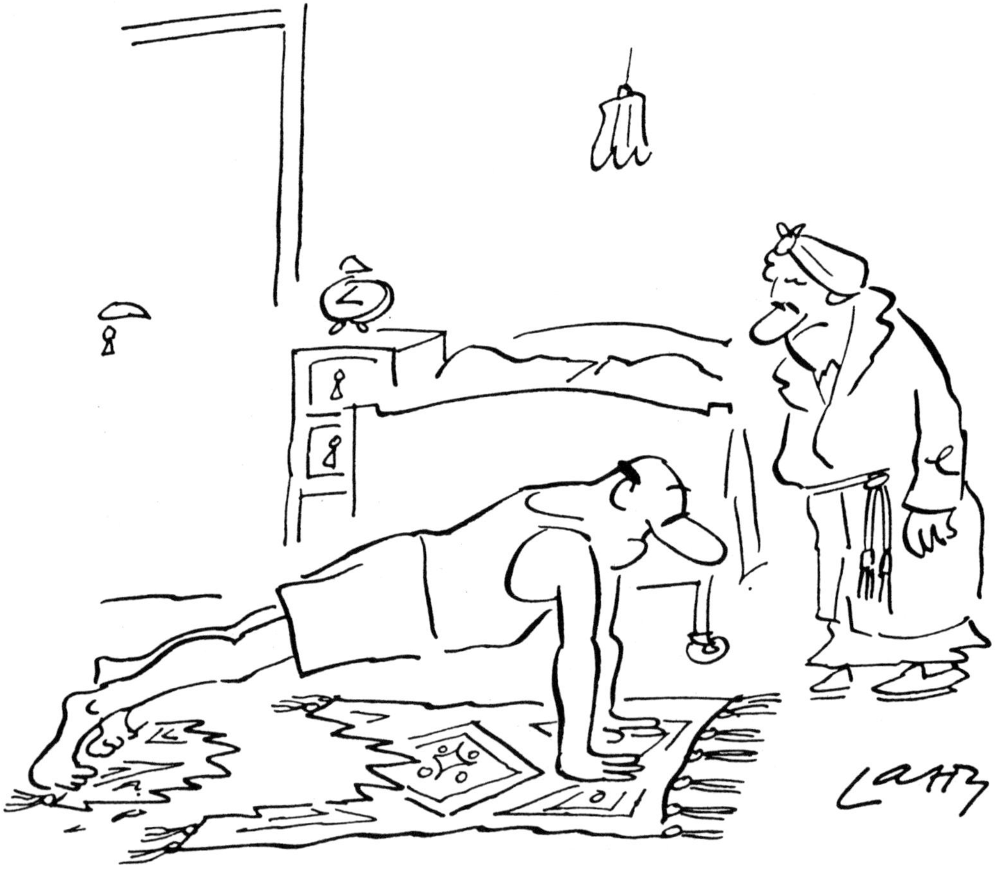

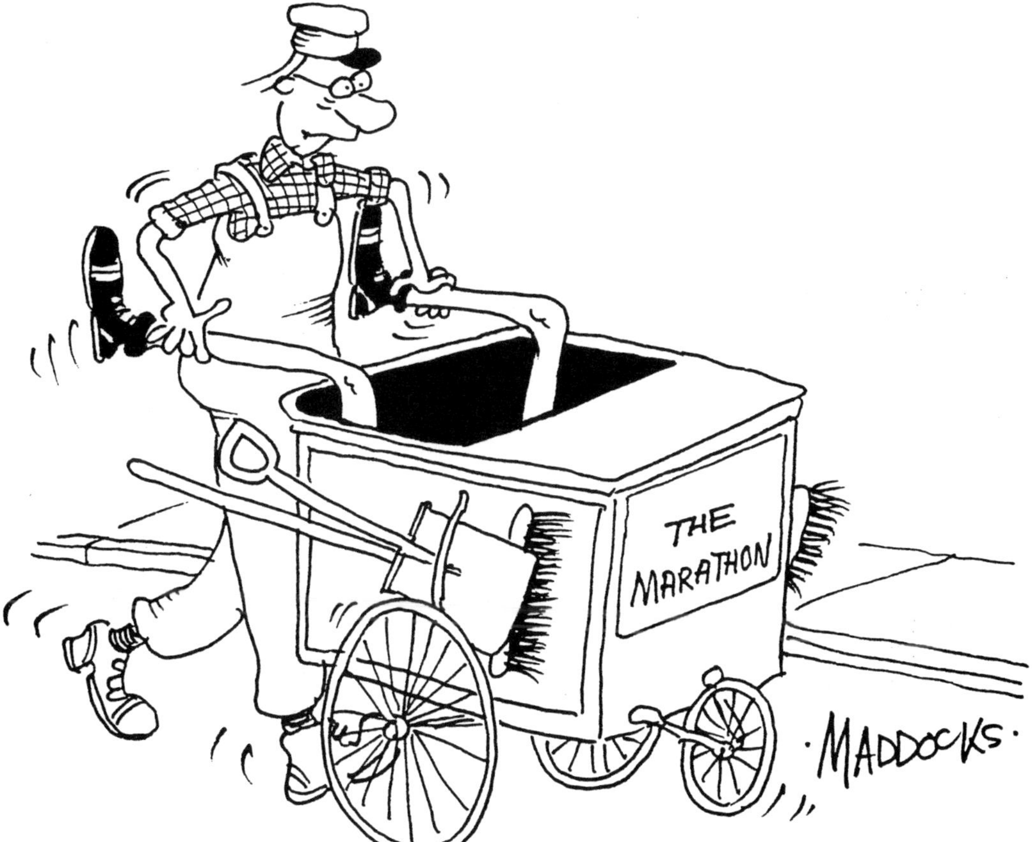
THE MARATHON
MADDOCKS

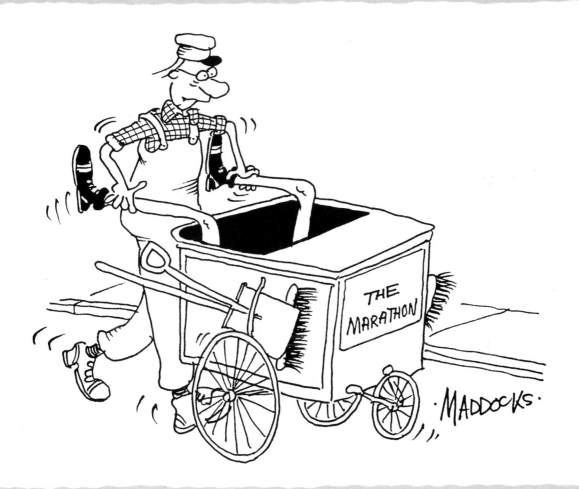

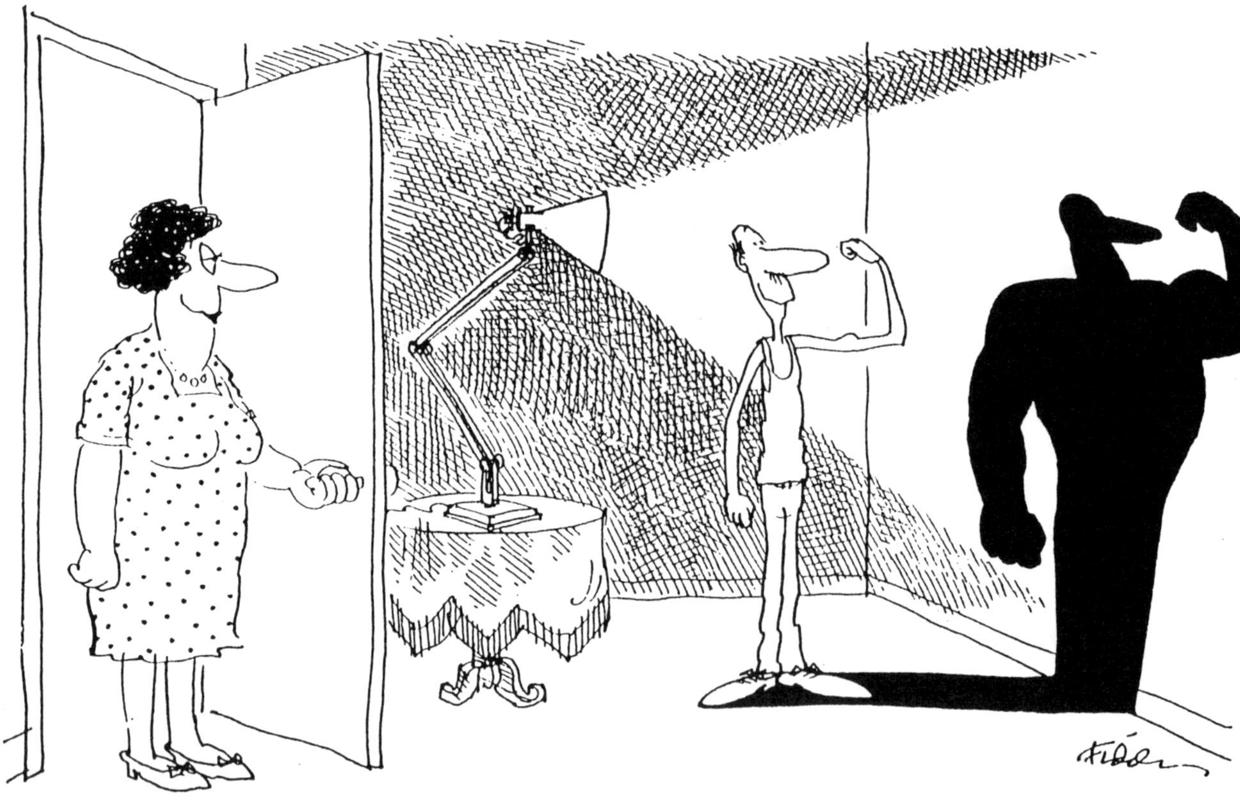

S. Nomano.

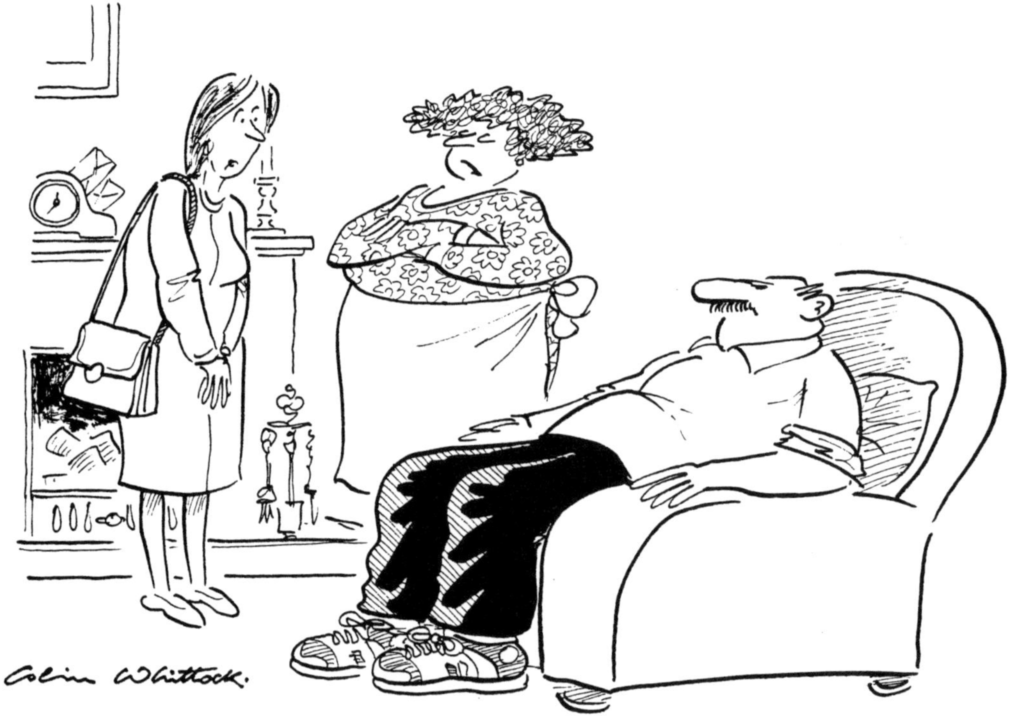
Colin Whittock.

"Bert believes in doing things gradually – today he tied the laces of his running-shoes . . ."

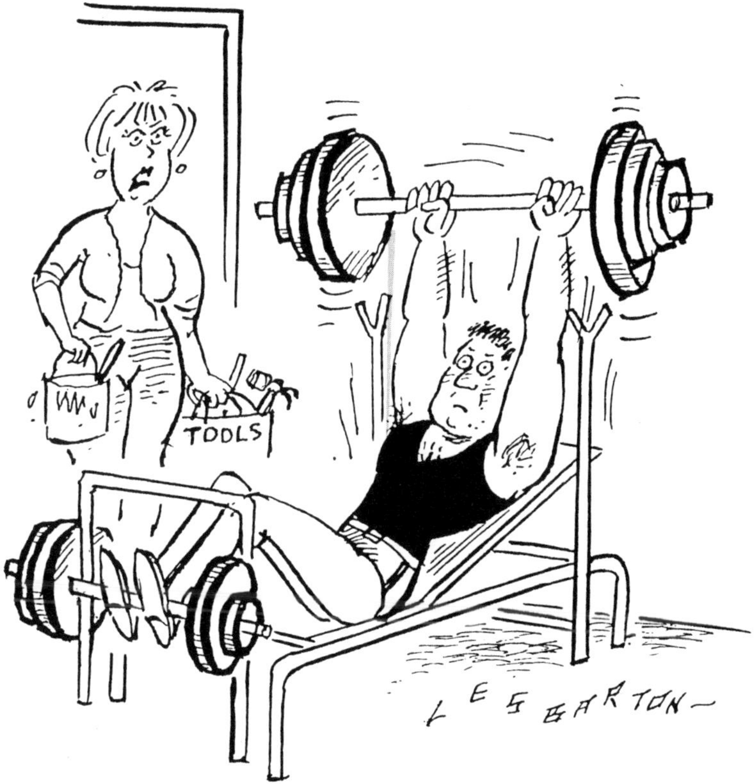
TOOLS
LES BARTON

"How come you're always too tired when I ask you to do something?"

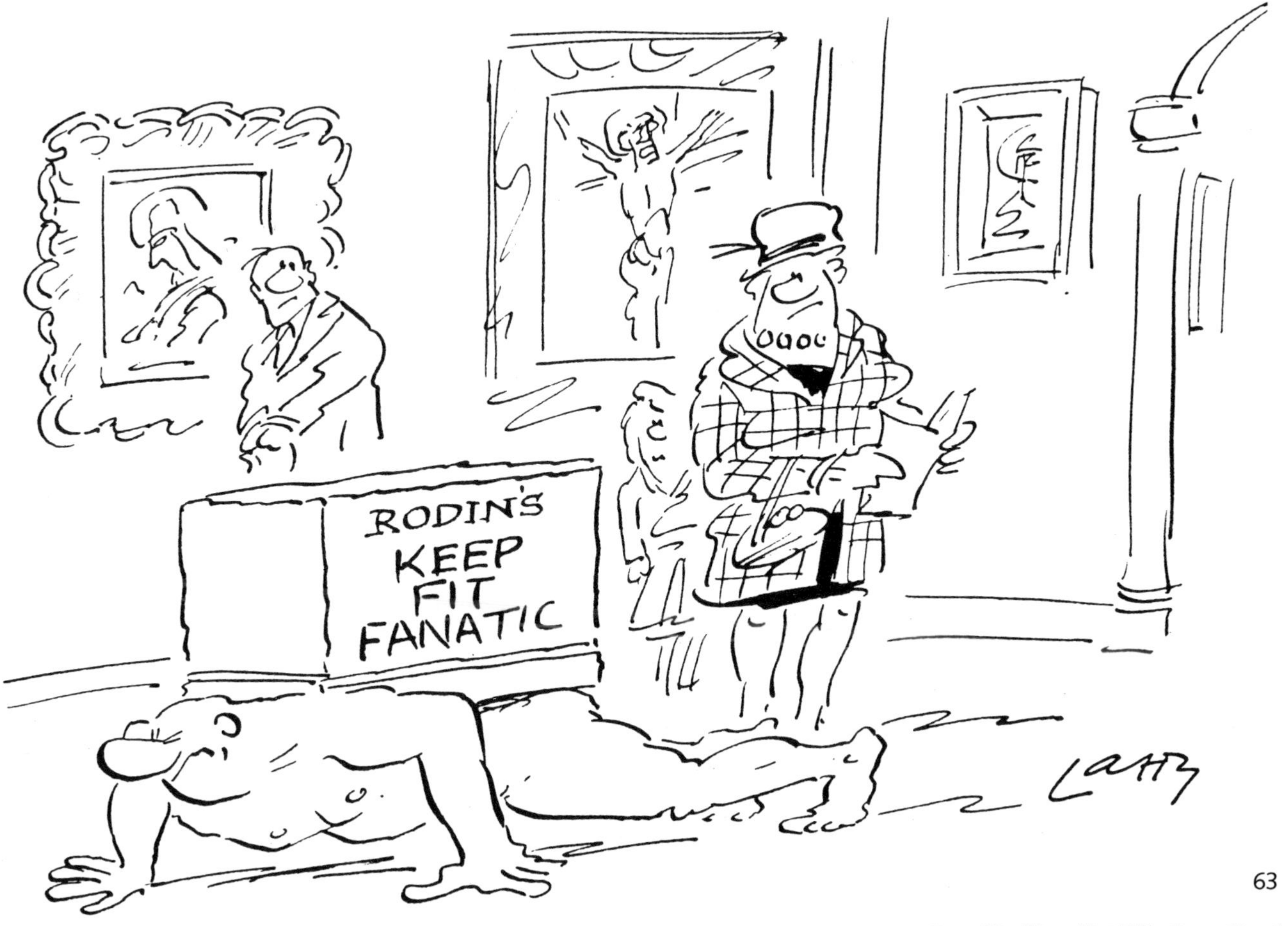
RODIN'S
KEEP
FIT
FANATIC
LARRY

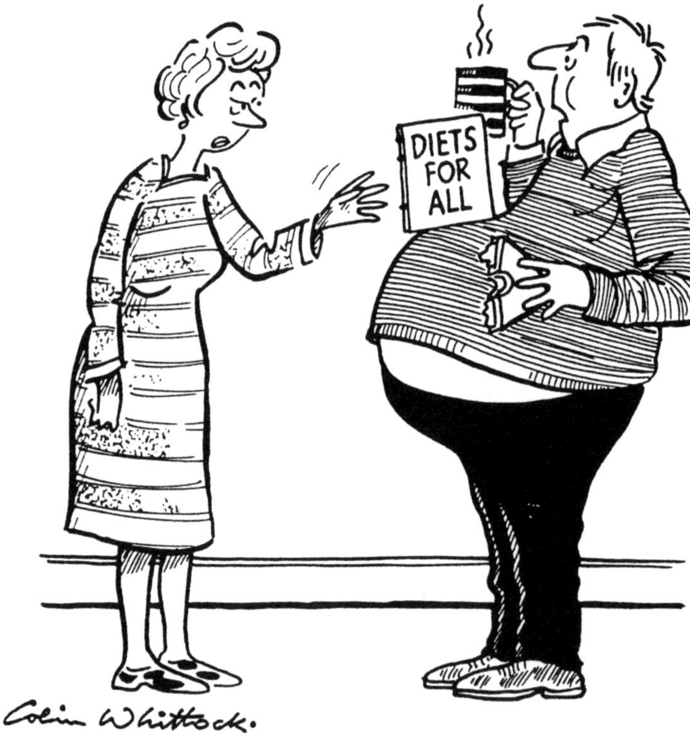
DIETS
FOR
ALL
Colin Whittock.

"It's all muscle!"

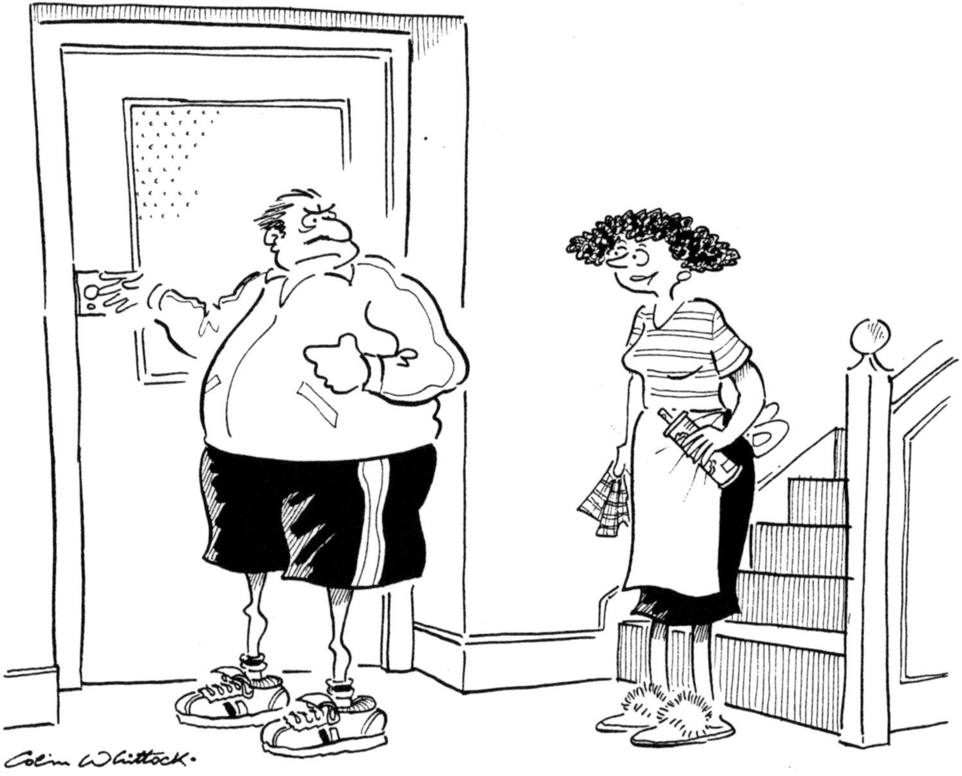
Colin Whittock.

"Pity you couldn't buy new legs to go with your running-shoes . . ."

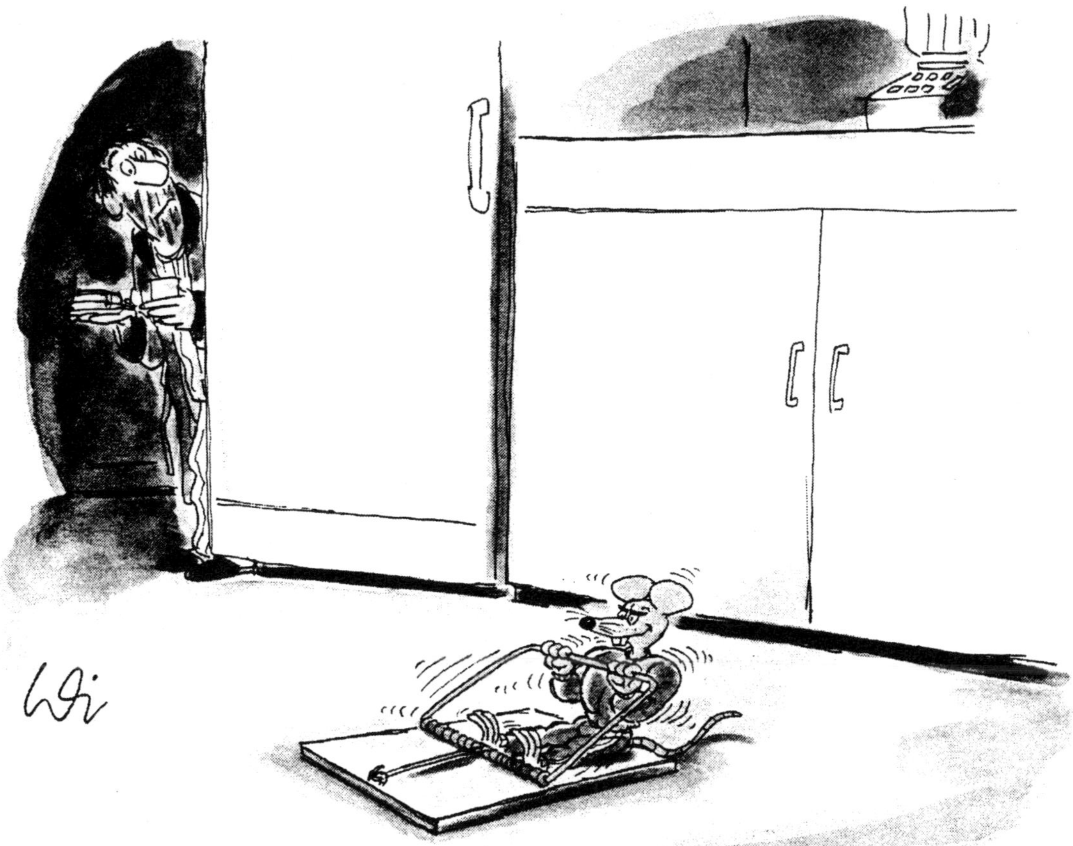

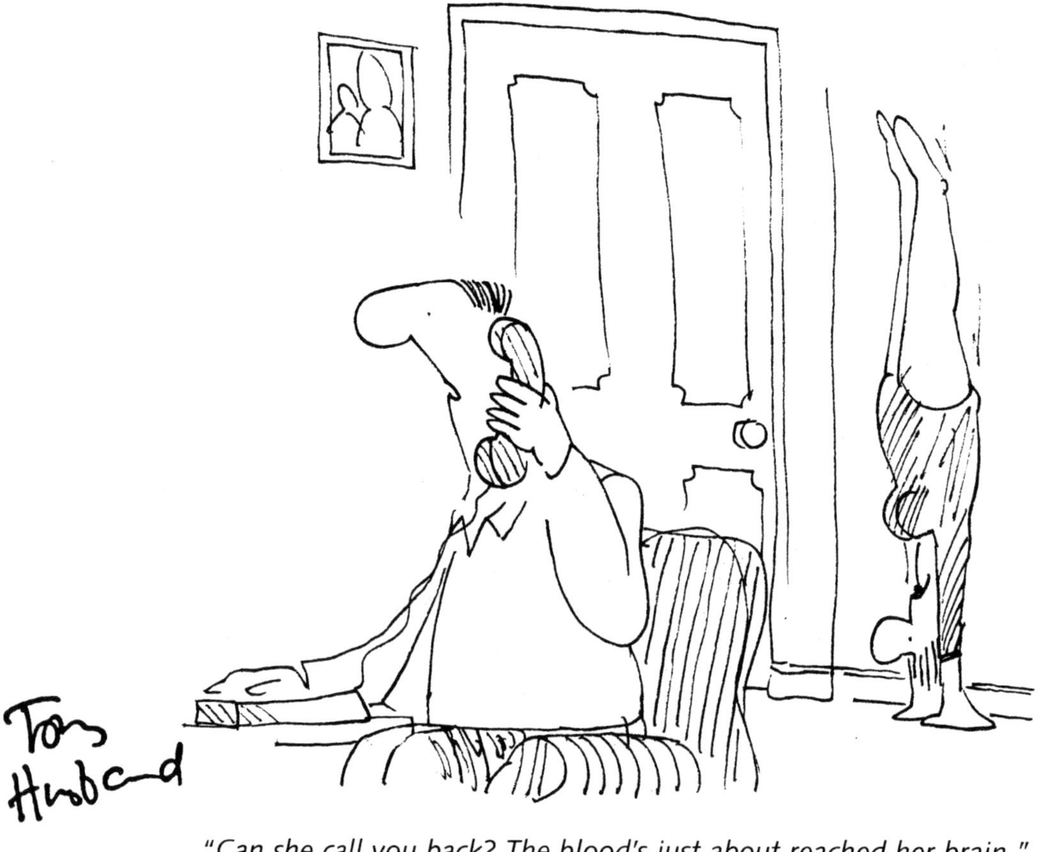
Tony Husband

"Can she call you back? The blood's just about reached her brain."

NIGEL SWEPT TINY BRENDA INTO HIS ARMS...
TRUE ROMANCE L. Ust.
Diet Coke
'MY GOD, WOMAN! YOU'RE A BAG OF BONES!' HE EXCLAIMED...
'PUT ON 140 POUNDS IMMEDIATELY - OR I'LL LEAVE YOU'.
I MADE ALL THAT UP, OF COURSE
©V.G

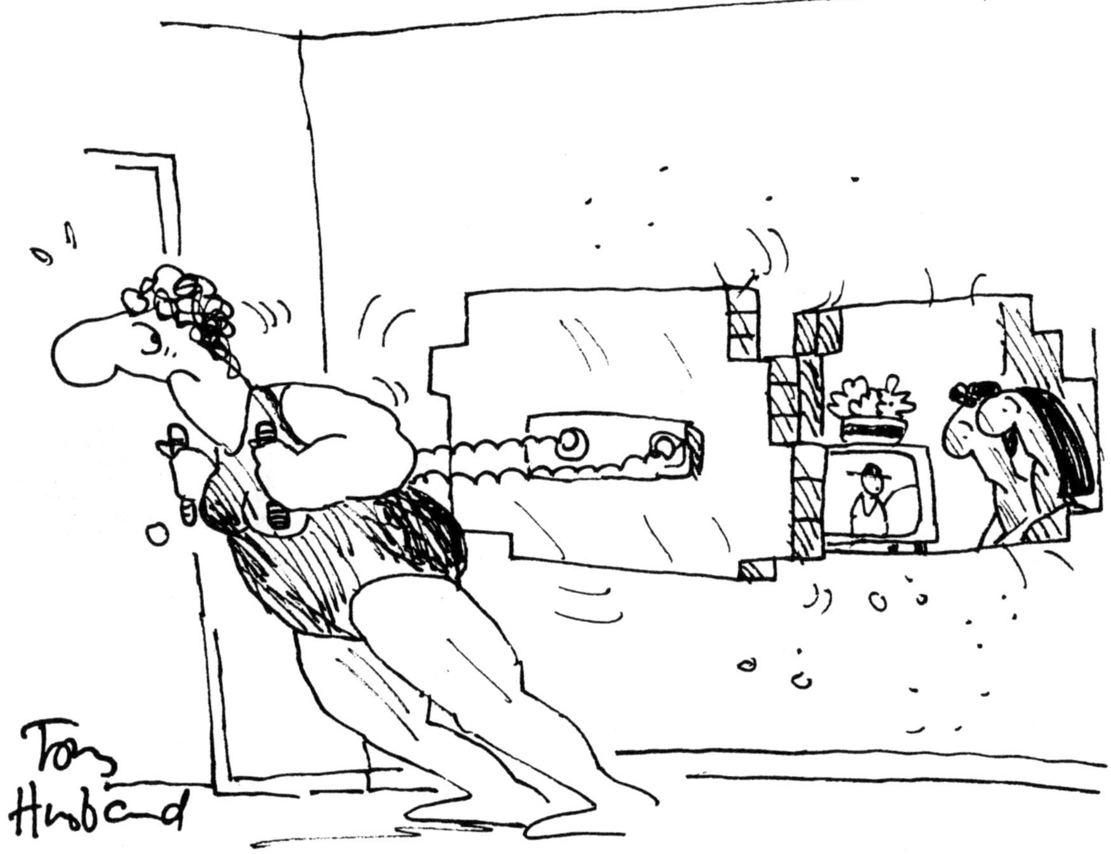
Tony Husband

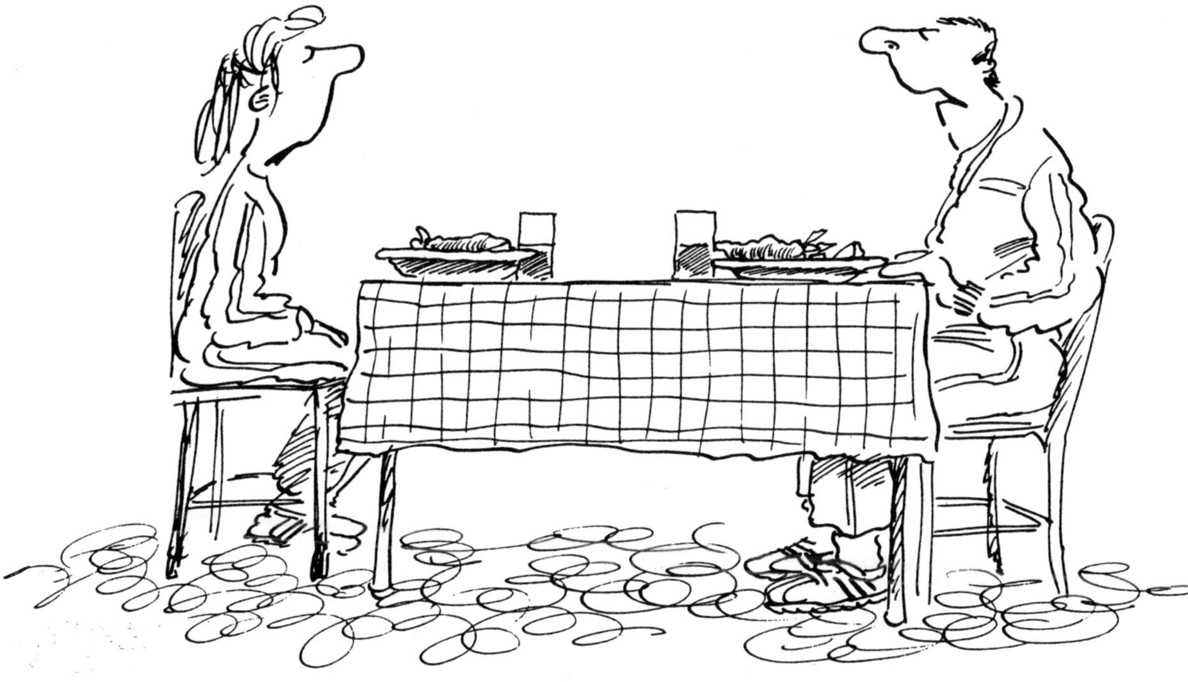

"Carrots! Jogging! Carrots! Jogging!
Do you think it's <u>worth</u> trying to prolong our lives?"

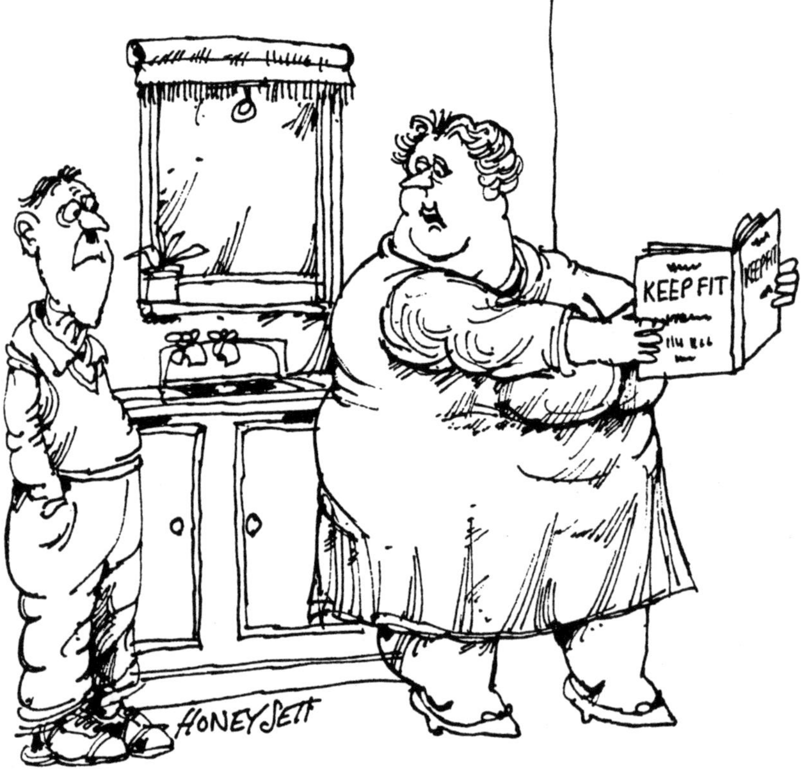
KEEP FIT
KEEP FIT
HONEYSETT

"The trouble is, I can't get close enough to read it!"

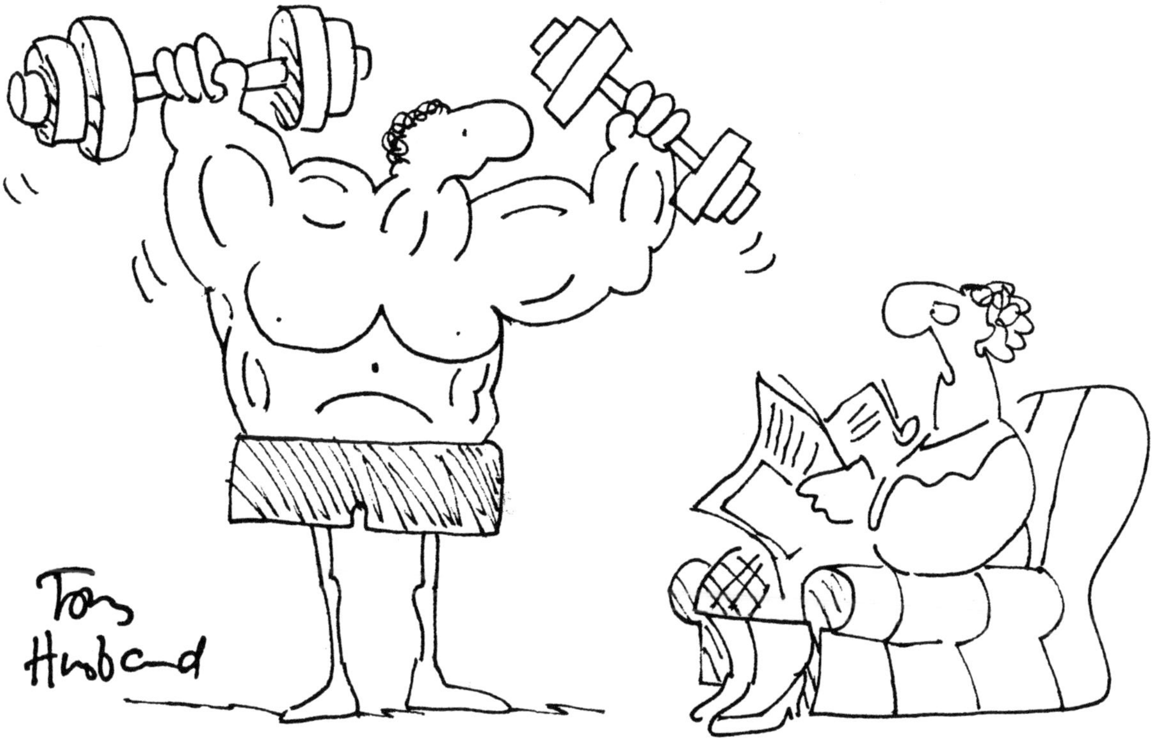

"Very good, but when do you start on the legs?"

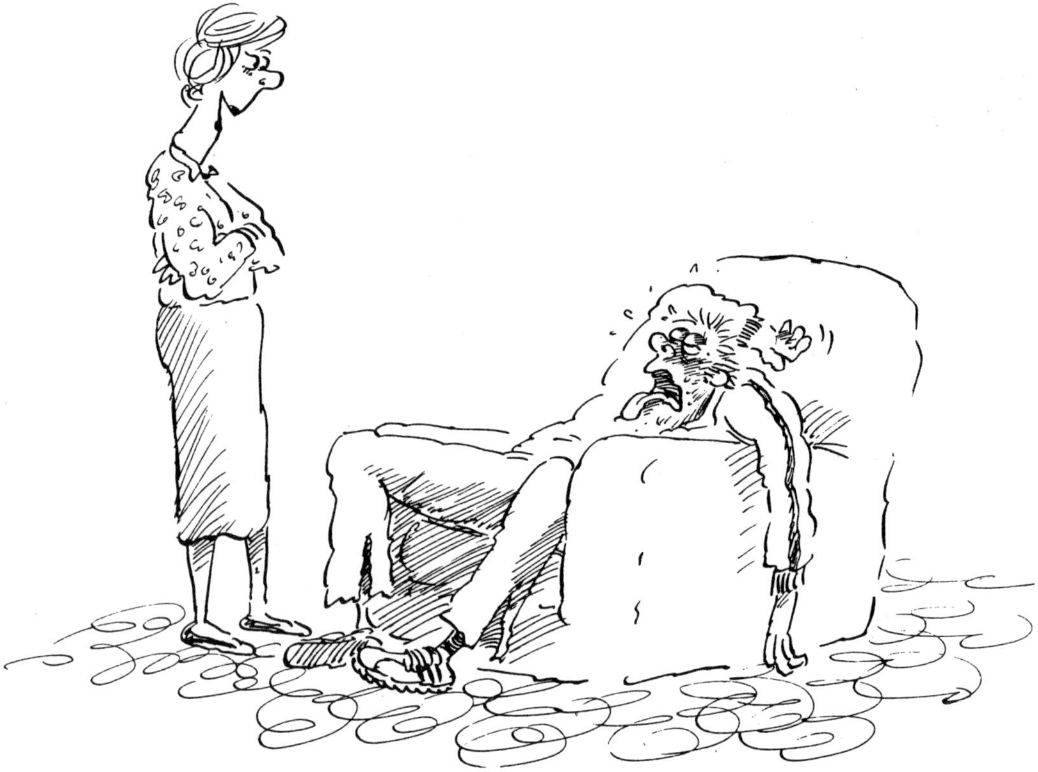

"All the way to the corner and back? Wow!"

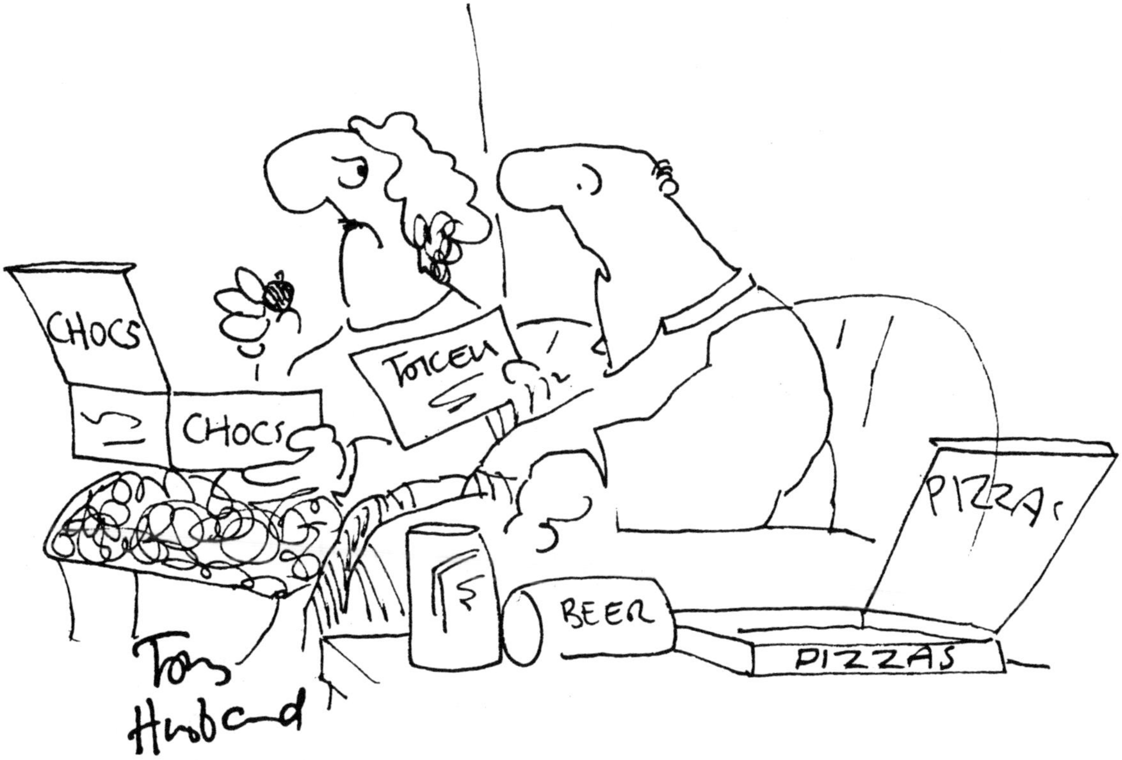
CHOCS
CHOCS
BEER
PIZZAS
Tony Husband

"We've got a free session at the local aerobics group."

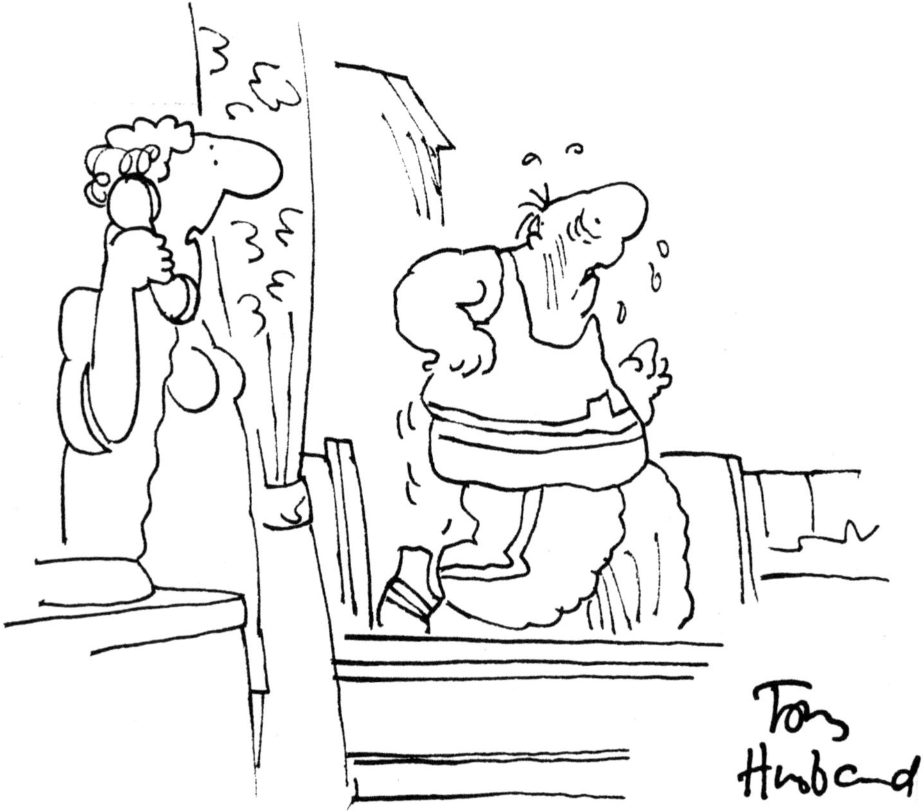

"Oh, hang on, Linford Christie's here now."

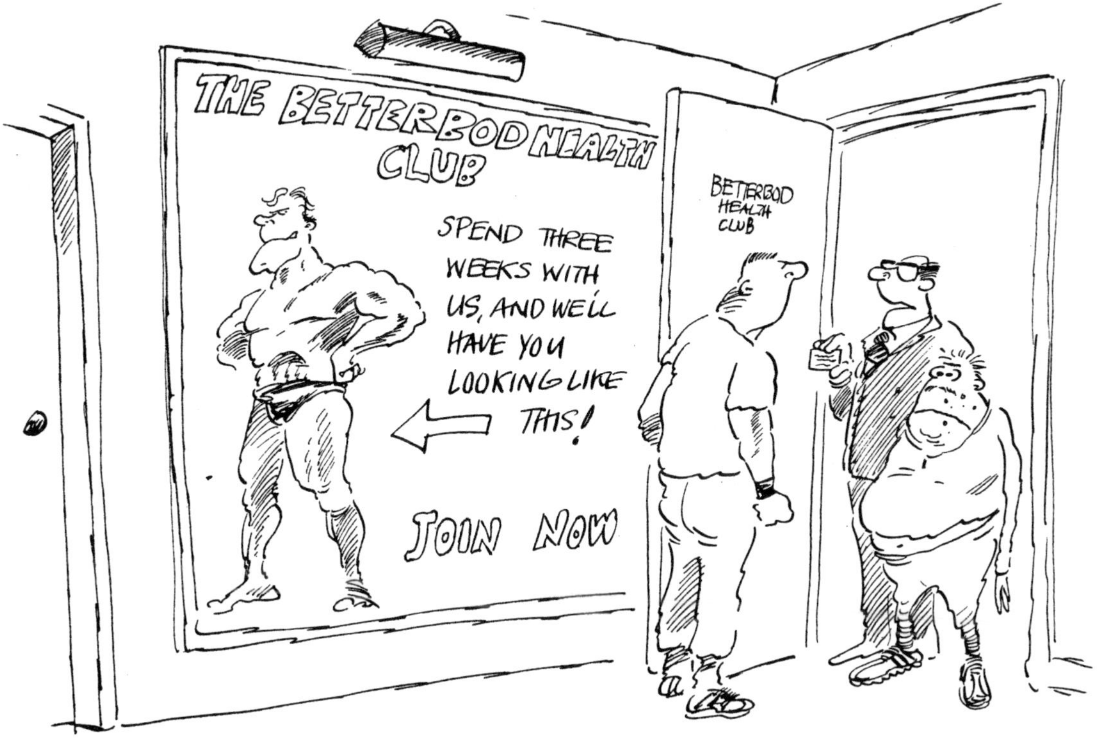
THE BETTERBOD HEALTH CLUB
SPEND THREE WEEKS WITH US, AND WE'LL HAVE YOU LOOKING LIKE THIS!
JOIN NOW
BETTERBOD HEALTH CLUB

"Good morning. I'm from the Consumer Report team.
I'd like a word with you about certain promises made to Mr Pratt here."

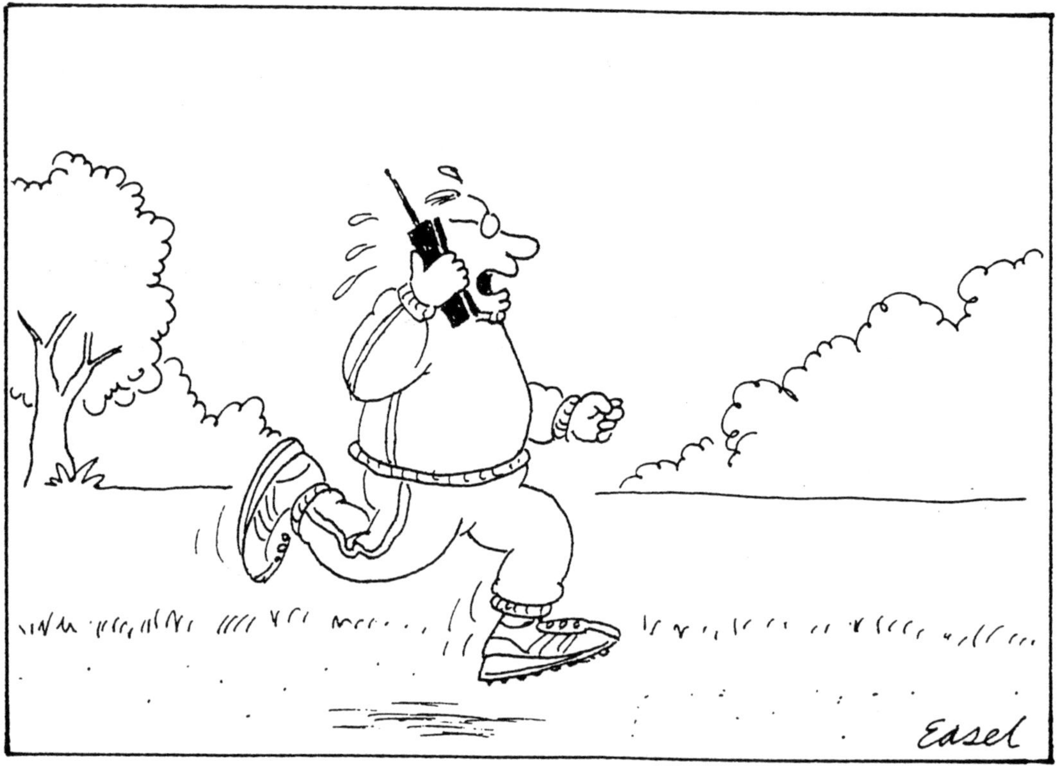
Easel

*"No, Miriam! . . . pant, pant . . . don't hang up . . . pant . . .
this isn't an obscene phone call."*

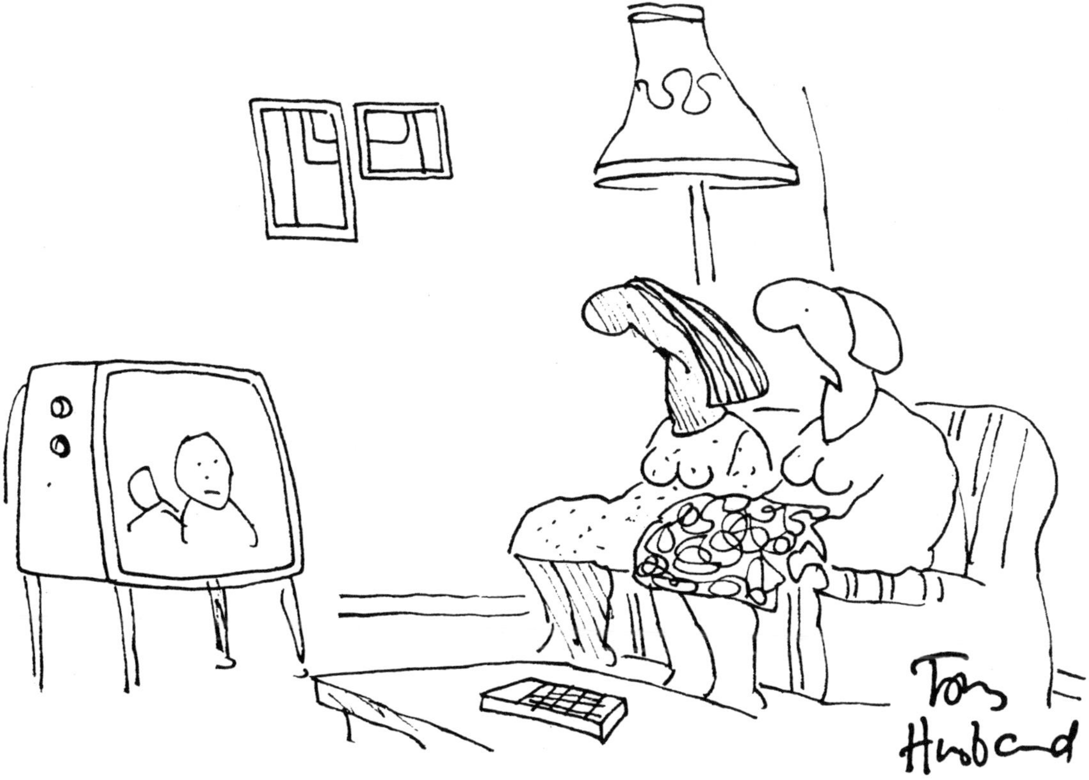

"I'd put the Jane Fonda keep-fit video on, but I can't reach the remote control."

Books in "The World's Greatest" series

($4.99 £2.99 paperback)
The World's Greatest Business Cartoons
The World's Greatest Cat Cartoons
The World's Greatest Computer Cartoons
The World's Greatest Dad Cartoons
The World's Greatest Do It Yourself Cartoons
The World's Greatest Golf Cartoons
The World's Greatest Keep-Fit Cartoons

Books in the "Victim's Guide" series

($4.99 £2.99 paperback)

Award winning cartoonist Roland Fiddy sees the funny side to life's phobias, nightmares and catastrophes.

The Victim's Guide to Air Travel
The Victim's Guide to the Baby
The Victim's Guide to Christmas
The Victim's Guide the Dentist
The Victim's Guide to the Doctor
The Victim's Guide to Middle Age

Books in the "Crazy World" series

($4.99 £2.99 paperback)
The Crazy World of Aerobics (Bill Stott)
The Crazy World of Cats (Bill Stott)
The Crazy World of Cricket (Bill Stott)
The Crazy World of Gardening (Bill Stott)
The Crazy World of Golf (Mike Knowles)
The Crazy World of The Handyman (Roland Fiddy)
The Crazy World of Hospitals (Bill Stott)
The Crazy World of Housework (Bill Stott)
The Crazy World of The Learner Driver (Bill Stott)

The Crazy World of Love (Roland Fiddy)
The Crazy World of Marriage (Bill Stott)
The Crazy World of Rugby (Bill Stott)
The Crazy World of Sailing (Peter Rigby)
The Crazy World of School (Bill Stott)
The Crazy World of Sex (Bill Stott)
The Crazy World of Soccer (Bill Stott)

Books in the "Fanatics" series

($4.99 £2.99 paperback)

The **Fanatic's Guides** are perfect presents for everyone with a hobby that has got out of hand. Eighty pages of hilarious black and white cartoons by Roland Fiddy.

The Fanatic's Guide to the Bed
The Fanatic's Guide to Cats
The Fanatic's Guide to Computers
The Fanatic's Guide to Dads
The Fanatic's Guide to Diets
The Fanatic's Guide to Dogs
The Fanatic's Guide to Husbands
The Fanatic's Guide to Money
The Fanatic's Guide to Sex
The Fanatic's Guide to Skiing
The Fanatic's Guide to Sports

Great Britain: Order these super books from your local bookseller or from Exley Publications Ltd. 16 Chalk Hill, Watford, Herts WDl 4BN. (Please send £1.30 to cover post and packaging on 1 book, £2.60 on 2 or more books.)